Literacy
Teacher's Book

Year 2

Louis Fidge

Letts
EDUCATIONAL

Acknowledgements

The authors and publisher are grateful for permission to reproduce the following text:

Abby by Wolfgang Hanel, translated by Rosemary Lanning © 1996 Nord-Süd Verlag AG Gossau Zürich/Schweiz

Helping by Lucy Coates, from *First Rhymes*, first published in UK in 1994 by Orchard Books, a division of the Watts Publishing Group, 96 Leonard Street, London EC2A 4RH

A Little Bit of Colour by Nancy Blishen, from *A Treasury of Stories for Five Year Olds* selected by E and N Blishen, published by Kingfisher, 1989

The Sick Young Dragon by John Foster © 1984 John Foster, first published in *A Very First Poetry Book* compiled by John Foster (Oxford University Press), included by permission of the author

The Snowy Day By Ezra Jack Keats © Ezra Jack Keats

Trees by Harry Behn from *Earthways* © Harry Behn

The Birthday Present by Charlotte Zolotow from *Mr Rabbit and the Lovely Present* © 1962 Charlotte Zolotow

The Giant's Accidents © Charles Thomson, from *Another First Poetry Book*, published by Oxford University Press

Mr Gumpy's Outing by John Burningham © John Burningham

When I Was One by A. A. Milne from the *Now We Are Six* collection © A. A. Milne, published by Ted Smart Publishers

Why do Dogs Chase Cars? from *South and North, East and West* edited text © 1992 Michael Rosen. Illustrations © 1992 Michael Foreman. Reproduced by permission of the publisher Walker Books Ltd., London

The Caterpillar by Marc Brown, from *Hand Rhymes* published by HarperCollins Publishers Ltd

Everybody Said No! by Sheila Lavelle, published by A&C Black (Publishers) Ltd

Cats by Michaela Miller is reprinted by permission of Heinemann Educational Publishers, a division of Reed Educational & Professional Publishing Ltd

The Story of Dr Dolittle by Hugh Lofting © Hugh Lofting and published by permission of the Estate of Hugh Lofting c/o Ralph M Vicinanza, Ltd

Winnie-the-Pooh by A. A. Milne, published by Methuen Children's Books (a division of Egmont Children's Books Limited). Illustrations published by permission of Curtis Brown.

Veterinary Surgeon by Christopher Maynard from *Jobs People Do*, published by Dorling Kindersley Ltd

Silly Ghosts Gruff by Michael Rosen from *Hairy Tales and Nursery Crimes*, published by Scholastic Children's Books

First published 1998, Reprinted 1999

Letts Educational, Schools and Colleges Division,
9–15 Aldine Street, London W12 8AW
Tel: 0181 740 2270   Fax: 0181 740 2280

Text © Louis Fidge

ISBN 1 84085 246 1

Designed by Gecko Limited, Bicester, Oxon
Produced by Ken Vail Graphic Design, Cambridge

Illustrated by Sarah Geeves, Sylvie Poggio Artists Agency (Bethan Matthews and Sarah Warburton), Judy Stevens, Simon Girling & Associates (Elizabeth Sawyer, Piers Harper, Sue King and Mark Ripley), David Lock, Blackman-Doyle (John Blackman), Graham-Cameron Illustration (Tim Archbold), Archer Art (Ross), Maggie Sayer, John Plumb, Joseph McEwan and Karen Donnelly

British Library Cataloguing-in-Publication Data
A CIP record for this book is available from the British Library

Printed in Great Britain by Ashford Colour Press, Gosport, Hants

Letts Educational is the trading name of BPP (Letts Educational) Ltd

CONTENTS

4–5	How to use the Poster Pack and Activity Books for the Literacy Hour
6–7	Scope and Sequence for the Activity Books
8–11	Scope and Sequence for the Poster Pack
12–13	Teacher's Planning Charts
14–15	Moira and Her Dog
16–17	Helping
18–19	A Little Bit of Colour
20–21	A Recipe for Gingerbread Men
22–23	The Sick Young Dragon
24–25	The Snowy Day
26–27	Trees
28–29	The School Visit
30–31	The Birthday Present
32–33	Helping Hedgehogs Hibernate
34–35	Enough for Two?
36–37	The Story of Milk
38–39	The Giant's Accidents
40–41	Mr Gumpy's Outing
42–43	Two Poems to Enjoy
44–45	An Animal Dictionary
46–47	Why Do Dogs Chase Cars?
48–49	The Caterpillar
50–51	Ma Liang and the Magic Brush
52–53	Rhymes Around the World
54–55	Everybody Said No!
56–57	The Brute Family
58–59	The Guest
60–61	Playing With Words
62–63	Animal Language
64–65	Winnie-the-Pooh
66–67	The Jungle Book
68–69	The Veterinary Surgeon
70–71	Using an Information Book
72–73	The Silly Ghosts Gruff
74–75	High Frequency Word List
76–80	Handy Hints for …

The Poster Packs:

- support the teaching of the Literacy Hour
- provide a major teaching/learning focus
- cover a wide range of types of literature, both fiction and non-fiction
- are useful for class, group or independent work
- contain teaching notes offering a wealth of practical ideas
- include activities and suggestions for Text, Sentence and Word Level work.

Teaching and learning strategies

The posters facilitate a wide range of teaching and learning strategies. They provide:

- a clear focus, allowing you to draw attention to and develop key strategies with the class
- opportunities to demonstrate skills, e.g. on how to read punctuation using a shared text
- opportunities for modelling, e.g. by discussing the features of the texts
- suggestions for scaffolding by offering support and structures for compositional writing
- the means to explain, clarify and discuss texts in a variety of ways at all three levels
- opportunities for questioning and probing understanding so pupils extend their ideas
- a means of initiating and guiding explorations into all areas of language, including grammar, spelling and meaning
- the means to investigate ideas and themes, e.g. to understand, expand on or generalise about underlying text structures
- opportunities to promote discussion and argument, encouraging pupils to voice their opinions, put forward their views, argue a case, or justify a preference
- a chance to develop speaking and listening skills, stimulating and extending pupils' contributions by discussion and evaluation.

Class activities – shared reading and writing

The posters may be used for a variety of purposes in a whole class situation. It is suggested that initially the text is read to the whole class, modelling good reading aloud, emphasising meaning and expression, paying due attention to the punctuation. The passage may be discussed for a variety of purposes.

- The posters may be used to extend reading skills and understanding. Activities may be selected from the Text Level suggestions for a variety of comprehension activities, encouraging children to read the lines, and between and beyond the lines.
- Similarly, the passage may be used as a platform for developing compositional writing. Activities may be selected from the writing comprehension menu. These may be chosen for a variety of reasons, e.g. for the purpose of promoting a class discussion, brainstorming ideas, planning, writing notes, etc., for subsequent use in a group session or as an independent activity.
- The passage on the poster may also be used as a basis for class work at Sentence Level, by selecting appropriate activities from either the 'grammatical awareness' section or the 'sentence construction and punctuation' section.
- At Word Level, the passages on the posters provide many opportunities for focusing on spelling or vocabulary work, by selecting appropriate activities from the relevant sections of the Teacher's Notes.

Guided group activities

The main difference in these sessions is that, whereas in the shared class sessions the emphasis is on modelling appropriate behaviour to the children, in these guided group sessions children are helped to develop their own *independent* reading and writing skills.

The posters are equally useful in the context of smaller group work, following on from the larger class activities. Having read the text previously with the class, it will now be more familiar and thus provide a valuable passage for practising developing reading skills. For example, the text could be read aloud for developing a greater awareness of phrasing, intonation, expression, attention to punctuation, etc. The text could be used for further comprehension activities from the suggestions in the Teacher's Notes, refining and developing children's abilities to use a variety of reading strategies and cues.

The posters may be used to develop writing tasks introduced earlier with the whole class, e.g. planning a piece of writing to be continued later, working on sentence construction activities, discussing ways of presenting an argument, etc.

Independent work

Independent work will be happening at the same time as the guided group work. A variety of forms of organisation are possible for this work. Independent work may be carried out within the context of ability groups operating on a carousel system, with a rotation of activities for each group during the week, or as completely individual work, e.g. a whole-class writing activity based on an earlier shared writing session.

In the shared class activities, the posters will have been used for a wide range of teaching objectives at any of the three levels of text, sentence or word work. The Teacher's Notes contain a comprehensive range of ideas which are suitable for independent work at each level, using the posters as a starting point. The posters, if not being used by other groups, could be available for reference purposes if necessary. The activities suggested are often not reliant on access to the poster at all.

Independent tasks could cover a wide range of objectives such as:

- independent reading and writing
- spelling activities and practice
- comprehension work
- vocabulary extension and dictionary or thesaurus work

- grammar, punctuation and sentence construction activities
- proof-reading and editing
- reviewing and evaluating work done, etc.

The plenary session

The posters provide an ideal focus for drawing sessions together. The session may be used to:

- refer back to and reinforce earlier teaching points by reference to the poster, helping pupils discuss, reflect upon and evaluate their work
- present pupils' work to the rest of the class
- assess what has been learned in the lesson
- flag up teaching points for future lessons
- praise and encourage achievements.

The relationship between the posters and the Letts Literacy Activity Books

The posters may be used entirely independently as a resource in their own right, as suggested above. However, to get maximum value from them, they are best used to complement the work in the Letts Literacy Activity Books. The stimulus passages on the posters are exactly the same as those which introduce each unit of work in the Activity Books. The activities are different, however. The combination of both Activity Books and ideas from the Poster Packs thus provides you with an even more extensive range of suggestions from which to select according to your individual situations and the needs of your class.

The texts themselves may be best introduced and discussed with the class, intially using the posters. Pupils could use the Activity Books as well, if you consider this appropriate. (The posters may, of course, also be used as a focus for small group and individual work, as suggested above.)

When not being specifically used as a teaching tool, individual posters could be pinned up in the classroom as part of your on-going classroom display, e.g. as the 'Poster of the week'.

UNIT	Title	Range
1.1	Moira and Her Dog	Story with a familiar theme and setting
1.2	Helping	Poem with a familiar theme and setting
1.3	A Little Bit of Colour	Story with a familiar theme and setting
1.4	A Recipe for Gingerbread Men	Instruction
1.5	The Sick Young Dragon	Poem with a familiar theme
1.6	The Snowy Day	Story with a familiar theme and setting
1.7	Trees	Poem with a familiar theme and setting
1.8	The School Visit	Plans and maps
1.9	The Birthday Present	Story with a familiar theme and setting
1.10	Helping Hedgehogs Hibernate	Instructions
	Glossary	
	High Frequency Word List	
2.1	Enough for Two?	Story from another culture
2.2	The Story of Milk	Explanation
2.3	The Giant's Accidents	Poem by a significant poet; poem with predictable language
2.4	Mr Gumpy's Outing	Story with patterned language
2.5	Two Poems to Enjoy	Poems by significant poets
2.6	An Animal Dictionary	Alphabetically ordered text
2.7	Why Do Dogs Chase Cars?	Traditional story from another culture
2.8	The Caterpillar	Poetry and explanation
2.9	Ma Liang and the Magic Brush	Traditional story from another culture; patterned language
2.10	Rhymes Around the World	Poems from other cultures
	Glossary	
	High Frequency Word List	
3.1	Everybody Said No!	Story by a significant children's author
3.2	The Brute Family	Story by a significant children's author
3.3	The Guest	Story by a significant children's author
3.4	Playing With Words	Texts with language play
3.5	Animal Language	Extended story
3.6	Winnie-the-Pooh	Stories by a significant children's author
3.7	The Jungle Book	Extended stories
3.8	Veterinary Surgeon	Non-chronological report
3.9	Using an Information Book	Information books
3.10	The Silly Ghosts Gruff	Texts with language play
	Glossary	
	High Frequency Word List	

Text Level	Sentence Level	Word Level
• Using a variety of cues to make sense of reading	Punctuating sentences	Long vowel digraphs
• Features of poetry	Reading for sense	Categorising words
• Making sense of reading, linking story to experience	Punctuation	Suffixing with 's', 'ing' and 'ed'
• Features of instructions	Sequencing instructions	Vowels and consonants
• Reasoning – features of poetry	Reading for sense	Word-building
• Story plot	Joining sentences – structural language	Phonemes – rhyming
• Features of poetry	Predicting word meanings	Vowels and phonemes
• Reading a plan	Using organisational devices	Phonemes
• Story plot	Punctuation, including capitals	Long vowels and digraphs
• Features of instructional texts	Predicting word meanings	Categorising words

Writing Focus   Writing a story; Writing a poem; Writing instructions.

Text Level	Sentence Level	Word Level
• Characterisation and settings	Subject/verb agreement; past tenses	Phonemes and antonyms
• Reading a flowchart	Sentence structure	Compound words
• Aspects of poetry	Grammatical sense	Vowel phonemes
• Characters, themes and settings	Speech marks	Vowel phonemes
• Aspects of poetry	Commas in lists	Vowel phonemes; consonant digraphs
• Alphabetical order; dictionaries	Grammatical sense	Syllables
• Characters and settings	Verb tenses	Prefixes 'un' and 'dis'; opposites
• Reading a flowchart; themes	Constructing simple sentences	Vowel phonemes
• Character and setting	Speech marks	Vowel phonemes
• Aspects of rhymes	Agreement	Rhyming

Writing Focus   Writing a story, poem and character profile; Using a glossary; Making a flowchart

Text Level	Sentence Level	Word Level
• Characterisation; oral retelling	Past tenses	Phonemes; suffixing with 'ing'
• Characterisation; settings	Commas in lists	Phoneme 'ea'
• Comparison with another author	Grammatical agreement	Words with the same spelling patterns/different sounds
• Responding to language play	Question marks	Thematic words; synonyms
• Characters; themes; comparison with another author	Questions	Suffixes 'ly' and 'ful'; digraphs
• Book blurbs	Turning statements into questions	Syllables
• Characters and settings	Standard forms of verbs	Spelling patterns
• Fiction/non-fiction; facts; use of headings	Posing questions	Thematic words; synonyms
• Contents page; index; glossary	Subject/verb agreement	Spelling strategies
• Evaluating text; comparing to original	Punctuation	Spelling strategies

Writing Focus   Finishing a story; Writing a story; Writing a nonsense verse; Writing an information text

	Poster	Range	Text Level
1.1	Moira and Her Dog	Story with a familiar theme and setting	Characters; Links with own experience; Using a variety of reading cues; Use of language; Settings; Descriptive writing
1.2	Helping	Poem with a familiar theme and setting	Links with own experience; Sequencing; Rhyming; Use of language; Reading and reciting poetry; Expressing personal opinions; Writing own poem; Story-writing
1.3	A Little Bit of Colour	Story with a familiar theme and setting	Predicting; Differences between an oral and a written story; Sequencing; What happened when … ; Continuing a story in own words; Writing about own experiences
1.4	A Recipe for Gingerbread Men	Instructions	Telling a story in own words; Features of instructional texts; Linking with personal experiences; Comparing texts; Sequencing; Writing instructions
1.5	The Sick Young Dragon	Poem with a familiar theme and setting	Prediction; Characters; What happened when …; Structure and features of a poem; Reading poetry; Writing about personal experiences; Poetry writing
1.6	The Snowy Day	Story with a familiar theme and setting	Links with personal experiences; Reasons for events; What happened when …; Use of language; Telling a story in own words; Comparing stories; Writing stories
1.7	Trees	Poem with a familiar theme and setting	Personal responses; Structure and features of a poem; Writing a poem; Writing facts
1.8	The School Visit	Plans and maps	Features of a plan; Riddles; Understanding and writing directions; Places of personal interest
1.9	The Birthday Present	Story with a familiar theme and setting	Prediction; Linking to personal experiences; Reading with expression; Dialogue; Setting; Writing letters
1.10	Helping Hedgehogs Hibernate	Instructions	Linking to personal experiences; Using cues in reading; Diagrams; Evaluating features of instructional texts; Writing explanations
2.1	Enough for Two?	Story from another culture	Setting; Characters; Writing a story in own words; Changing the setting of story
2.2	The Story of Milk	Explanation	Reading a flow chart explaining process; Prediction; Using captions; Explaining in own words; Writing an explanation of a process
2.3	The Giant's Accidents	Poem by significant poet, with predictable language	Prediction; Links with experience; Features of a poem; Use of language; Extending a poem in own words
2.4	Mr Gumpy's Outing	Story with patterned language	Prediction; Characters; Use of patterned language; Key words; expressing personal opinions; Characters
2.5	Two Poems to Enjoy	Poems by significant poets	Expressing personal opinions; Poets; Features of poems; Comparison of poems; Extending poems; Collecting poems

Sentence Level	Word Level
Use of grammatical cues; Commas	Word-making; Vowels and consonants; Alphabetic knowledge; Topic words
Use of linking words and phrases; Commas	Suffixing with 'ing'; High frequency words; Classifying words
Using grammatical cues when reading; Effect of punctuation when reading; Use of capital letters	Phonemes; Words with the same letter patterns/different sounds; Explaining unfamiliar words; Compound words
Linking words and phrases; Organisational and presentational devices	Vowels and consonants; Vowel phonemes; Spelling strategies; Classifying words
Linking and structuring words; Effect of punctuation when reading	Plurals; Suffixing with 'ed'; Spelling strategies; Topic words
Joining sentences with simple conjunctions; Use of capital letters for proper nouns; Exclamation marks	Plurals; Suffixing with 'ing' and 'ed'; Topic words; Alphabetical order
Using grammatical cues when reading; Using commas in poetry	Word-building and making; Topic words
Use of grammatical knowledge when reading; Making a plan; Using organisational devices	Vowels; Spelling
Use of sequencing and linking words; Speech marks	Double consonants and double vowels; High frequency words; Classifying words
Using grammatical knowledge when reading; Labelling using arrows; Flow diagrams	Letter patterns; Linking pairs of words by association
Taking grammar and punctuation into account when reading; Reading for sense and accuracy; Speech marks	Syllables; Writing proper nouns; Alphabetical order
Subject/verb agreement; Writing proper sentences	Consonant digraphs; Words derived from people's names
Taking grammar and punctuation into account when reading; Irregular past tenses; Commas in lists	Compound words; Thematic words; Language play
Using past tenses correctly; Speech marks; Question marks	Prefixes; Antonyms
Taking grammar and punctuation into account when reading; Subject/verb agreement; Using commas in poetry	Syllables; Colour words; Shades of meaning

	Poster	Range	Text Level
2.6	An Animal Dictionary	Alphabetically ordered texts	Use of alphabetically ordered texts; Layout and organisation of dictionaries; Definitions; Writing explanations; Making a class dictionary
2.7	Why Do Dogs Chase Cars?	Traditional story from another culture	Prediction; Characters; Settings; Retelling in own words; Role play; Using story structure for own writing
2.8	The Caterpillar	Poetry and explanatory text	Comparing different types of text with the same theme; Flow diagrams; Rhymes; Writing a poem
2.9	Ma Liang and the Magic Brush	Traditional story from another culture, with patterned language	Setting; Characters; Events; Predicting; Personal opinions; Writing in own words; Character profile
2.10	Rhymes Around the World	Poems/rhymes from other cultures	Settings; Patterns of rhythm, rhymes and features of sounds; Language of poems; Extending rhymes; Collecting rhymes
3.1	Everybody Said No!	Story by a significant children's author	Comparing stories with similar themes; Knowledge of authors; Prediction; Expressing opinions; Continuing a story
3.2	The Brute Family	Story by a significant children's author	Characters; Setting; Personal opinions; Comparing stories with similar themes; Continuing a story; Character profiles
3.3	The Guest	Story by a significant children's author	Setting; Prediction; Comparing stories; Writing a review; Writing rules
3.4	Playing With Words	Texts with language play	Humorous words and phrases; Sound words; Types of poems; Writing own riddles, tongue twisters and nonsense rhymes
3.5	Animal Language	Extended story	Reading part of an extended story; Authors; Comparing a book with a film; Setting; Characters; Plot; Dialogue; Stories with the same theme; Continuing a story
3.6	Winnie-the-Pooh	Stories by a significant children's author	Knowledge of authors; Book blurbs; Authorship and publication
3.7	The Jungle Book	Extended story	Reading part of an extended story; Authors; Setting; Stories with similar themes; Writing sequels
3.8	Veterinary Surgeon	Non-chronological report	Posing questions prior to reading; Scanning, skimming and close-reading a text; Facts; Fiction/non-fiction; Evaluating a text; Notes; Non-chronological reports
3.9	Using an Information Book	Information books	Familiarisation with aspects of information books – contents, indexes, glossaries; Writing a review; Evaluating the usefulness of a text
3.10	The Silly Ghosts Gruff	Texts with language play	Comparing stories with similar themes; Humorous words and phrases; Use of language play; Story language; Author; Writing nonsense sentences and rhymes

Sentence Level	Word Level
Reading for sense and accuracy; Different ways of reading texts; Sentence structure	Common word endings; Proof-reading; Spelling strategies; Alphabetical order; Definitions
Correct use of past tense; Commas in lists	Phonemes; Letter patterns; Homophones; Antonyms
Subject/verb agreement; Use of proper sentences	Compound words; Proper nouns
Subject/verb agreement; Sentence structure and punctuation	Suffixing with 'ing' and 'ed'; Synonyms; Antonyms
Reading for sense and coherence; Punctuation – full stops, commas, question and exclamation marks	Compound words; Suffixing with 'ful'; Antonyms
Correct use of verb tenses; Dialogue; Questions; Proper nouns	Compound words; Synonyms
Subject/verb agreement (using pronouns); Punctuating sentences	Suffixing with 'ful' and 'ly'; Synonyms
Reading with appreciation of grammar and punctuation; Different forms of questions	Word-making; Comparing phonemes; Antonyms
Reading for sense; Lists using commas	Rhyming; Using a dictionary; Alliteration
Subject/verb agreement; Questions	Spelling strategies; Thematic words
Using past tenses appropriately; Questions	Letter patterns; Definitions; Thematic words
Reading for sense; Punctuating sentences	High frequency words; Suffixing; Categorising words; Synonyms
Grammatical agreement using pronouns; Writing questions	Spelling strategies; Thematic words
Subject/verb agreement; Lists using commas	Phonemes; Making a glossary; Word definitions; Alphabetical order
Sense and coherence; Proper nouns	Suffixing with 'ly'; Synonyms; Antonyms

Weekly Planner for the Literacy Hour

Week beginning:

(Using Letts Poster Packs, Literacy Activity Books,
Differentiated Activity Books for Sentence and Word Level)

	Class		Year Group(s)		Term	Teacher
	Whole class – shared reading and writing	Whole class – phonics, spelling, vocabulary and grammar	Guided group tasks (reading or writing)	Guided group tasks (reading or writing)	Independent group tasks	Plenary
Mon						
Tues						
Wed						
Thur						
Fri						

Termly Planner for the Literacy Hour

Term

(Using Letts Poster Packs, Literacy Activity Books,
Differentiated Activity Books for Sentence and Word Level)

Class		Year Group(s)		Teacher	

	Text Level	Sentence Level	Word Level	Texts: Titles and Range	WEEK NUMBER
1					
2					
3					
4					
5					
6					
7					
8					
9					
10					

Moira and Her Dog

About the text

Abby the dog is black with white patches –
and she's the nicest dog in the world. This
extract is about a small girl, Moira, and her
dog, and is taken from a story with a familiar
theme and setting.

Teaching opportunities at:

TEXT Level
Reading comprehension

1 Read the title and look together at the
illustration. Discuss the picture. Talk about the
girl and the dog. Describe them. Discuss what
they are doing and why they might be sitting
on the cliff edge. *(This discussion is open-ended,*
and will depend on the children's interpretation
of the picture.) Ask the children to suggest any
possible dangers in doing this. *(Answers will*
depend on the children's interpretation.)

2 Read the title again. What is the girl's name?
(Moira.) What is the dog's name? *(Abby.)*
Ask the children who have dogs as pets to
talk about their dogs – their names, habits,
the sorts of things they get up to, the fun
they have together – as well as the
responsibilities of caring for and looking
after their pets.

3 Read the passage to and with the children,
using phonological, contextual, grammatical
and graphic knowledge to work out the
meanings of unfamiliar words, for example,
'perplexed', 'driftwood' and 'spray', and to
make sense of what they read.

4 Ask the children what more they have found
out about Moira (where she lives, what she
likes doing) and Abby (what his job is, what
he does with Moira). *(Moira lives in a house*

on an island by the seaside. Abby's job is to
watch the goats.)*

5 Moira lives on an island. Ask the children to
explain what this means. *(An island is a piece*
of land surrounded by sea. Point out that Great
Britain is an island.) Discuss any occasions
when they have been to the seaside. What sort
of things do they like doing? Have they ever
collected shells or seen cliffs?

6 Discuss the way the author describes the
waves crashing against the cliffs and the
rocks. Ask the children to volunteer some
sound words associated with water, such as
'splash', 'crash' and 'splosh'. *(This will be an*
open-ended discussion.)

7 How is it possible to tell Moira likes animals
from the story? *(Her dog loves her and she*
likes the birds to come to sit on her hands.)

Key Stage 1
Literacy Poster Pack 2
Letts EDUCATIONAL

Moira and Her Dog

Moira has a dog called Abby.
Abby is black with white patches,
and she's the nicest dog in the world.
Abby's job is to watch the goats and
make sure they don't run away.
She keeps the cats out of the house too.
Abby is Moira's best friend.
  They often go to the meadow together
and watch the clouds floating past and the
seagulls wheeling and diving. This makes Moira
and Abby dizzy after a while. Then they have to
look away.
  Sometimes they run down to the beach to look
for driftwood and unusual shells. Or they walk
to the other end of the island. There the cliffs
are high and steep, and the waves send
up huge fountains of spray as they
crash against the rocks. Moira
and Abby sit on the highest cliff, and
Moira shouts and waves when a fishing boat sails by.
  Moira can sit perfectly still, holding out her arms like
the branches of a tree. Then little birds come and
sit on her hands or on her head. Abby
sits beside her, looking perplexed.
From Abby
by Wolfram
Hanel

© Letts Educational 1998   See *Letts Literacy Activity Book 2 Term 1* page 6

Writing comprehension

1 Ask the children to write a description either of a pet they own or about an imaginary one. Encourage them to describe how it looks, what sort of things it does, what it likes to eat, how it has to be looked after, etc.

2 Suggest they write about a real or imagined adventure they have with their pet, or to write about an adventure Moira might have with Abby.

SENTENCE Level
Grammatical awareness

1 Decide upon a particular part of speech to focus on, e.g. nouns, verbs, adjectives, etc., and select a number of sentences from the passage. Write the sentences out but omit the selected part of speech. Ask the children to fill in the missing words. This will help focus on a particular type of word and on using grammatical cues while reading. *(Answers will depend on the section and part of speech chosen.)*

Sentence construction and punctuation

1 Ask the children to look for commas in the passage. Find and read the sentences, discussing the need to pause at each comma. *(See line 2, line 15, line 20, line 18, line 20 and line 23.)* Suggest the children hold a 'comma' hunt and to see how many commas they can find in a given text.

WORD Level
Spelling

1 Starting with a given word from the text, encourage the children to do the following word-building activities. Change the 'l' in 'look' to 'b', 'c', 'h', 'r', 't', 'cr' and 'br'. Change the 'w' in 'wood' to 'g', 'h', and 'st'. Change the 'd' in 'down' to 'g', 't', 'cr', 'br', 'cl', 'fr' and 'dr'. Change the 'sh' in 'shout' to 'ab', 'cl', 'st'. *('Wood': 'good', 'hood', 'stood'; 'down': 'gown', 'town', 'crown', 'brown', 'clown', 'frown', 'drown'; 'shout': 'about', 'clout', 'stout'.)*

2 Select a number of words from the text and ask them to circle all the vowels in them. Discuss the fact that there are five vowels (a, e, i, o, u – and one 'part-time' vowel, y). All the other letters are called consonants.

3 Ask them to write the alphabet and colour in all the vowels.

Vocabulary extension

1 Use the text as a basis for collecting words to do with the seaside. Brainstorm this with the children and write other words they suggest on the board. If appropriate, arrange them in alphabetical order according to first letters.

Related texts

Further stories with an island setting:

'The Katie Morag' series by Mairi Hedderwick –

'Katie Morag and the Wedding'

'Katie Morag and the Two Grandmothers'

'Katie Morag Delivers the Mail'

Stories of a girl goatherder:

'Heidi' by Johanna Spyri

Helping

About the text

This poem is about helping parents at home with the chores – washing, cleaning the car, helping in the kitchen, gardening, shopping and so on.

Teaching opportunities at:

TEXT Level
Reading comprehension

1 Read the title and look at the illustrations. Ask the children to suggest ways they themselves help at home. What sort of jobs do they do? Allow this to lead on to a wider discussion of the duties and responsibilities of being in a family. Does everyone have a responsibility to help? Are there jobs that only women should do? Are there jobs that only men should do? *(This should engender lively debate!)*

2 Read the poem through with the children. Ask them to list the sequence of jobs done and which parent was involved in doing them. *(The laundry with Mum, cleaning the car with Dad, making the lunch with Mum, washing up with Dad, gardening with Mum and shopping with Dad.)*

3 Read the poem through again, stressing its rhythmic nature as you do so. Then read it a third time, this time pausing before the last word at the end of every other line, encouraging children to provide the missing rhyming word.

4 Read the poem in sections and discuss any interesting aspects of each one. For example, in the first section draw attention to the 'sound' words associated with water. *('Splish, splash, sploshing'.)* Point out the fact that every other line rhymes. *(They are rhyming couplets.)* Ask why it says 'Wind must blow and sun must shine'.

5 Encourage the children to reread the poem several times and recite it to others.

6 Look in anthologies for other poems about helping around the house. Read and compare these, asking the children to voice their opinions on what they liked or disliked about each.

Writing comprehension

1 Use the poem structure as a model. As a class, brainstorm some other jobs around the house, such as making the beds, sweeping up, clearing the table, etc. Ask the children to suggest words, phrases and sentences associated with each. (Use this as an opportunity to practise and reinforce spelling.) Discuss how some of these may be used and moulded into further lines for the poem.

2 Ask the children to make up a funny story about something unusual that happened when they helped at home. For example, the day the broom wouldn't stop sweeping, or the 'off' switch of the vacuum cleaner got stuck.

SENTENCE Level
Grammatical awareness

1 Revisit the sequence of events in the poem. Ask the children to write a simple sentence about each, and to use words like 'first', 'then', 'after this', 'lastly', etc., to link the sentences and structure the writing.

Sentence construction and punctuation

1 Encourage the children to read the poem, recognising and taking into account any punctuation, especially the commas, that helps with phrasing and expression.

WORD Level
Spelling

1 Look for words in the poem ending in '-ing'. *('Sploshing', 'helping', 'washing' and 'drying'.)* Point out how these consist of a root word plus the suffix, so 'help + ing'. Select some more verbs from the poem to which '-ing' may be added without changing the root word. *(These are: 'splish', 'splash', 'blow', 'hang', 'spray', 'clean', 'peel', 'crunch', 'go', 'clink', 'clank', 'pull' and 'sow'.)* Ask the children to make these into '-ing' words.

2 Look in other reading books and list other '-ing' words. If appropriate, identify the root word from which each arises. This could lead to a discussion of words in which the final 'e' is dropped, as with 'make', or the final letter is doubled, as with 'hop'.

3 Use the poem for a 'high frequency word' hunt. List some of the High Frequency Words from pages 74–75. Ask the children to see how many they can spot in the poem.

Vocabulary extension

1 Encourage the children to list as many jobs as they can that need doing around the house. Find different ways of classifying these, perhaps into indoor jobs, jobs in the garden, jobs involving cleaning, jobs involving water, jobs involving tools or machines, hard and easy jobs, and so on.

Related texts

Other poetry by Lucy Coates:

'First Rhymes: A Day of Rhymes, Games and Songs'

'One Hungry Baby, A Bedtime Counting Rhyme'

Books about helping:

'I'll Do It' by Brian Moses and Mike Gordon

A Little Bit of Colour

About the text

Tom and Daniel had a wonderful idea. Why not paint the greenhouse? At least, it seemed a good idea until Daniel's mum came down into the garden to bring them a drink!

Key Stage 1
Literacy Poster Pack 2
Letts EDUCATIONAL

A Little Bit of Colour

A wonderful idea popped into Daniel's head. 'Tom, why don't we paint the greenhouse? Not white like it is now, but all the colours of the rainbow?' he said.

'GREAT!' exclaimed Thomas, and they went into the cellar to collect paint and brushes. On a shelf they found a row of half-empty paint tins – blue, green, orange, yellow and red. They carried these down to the greenhouse and started work.

'Let's paint the doors orange and the window frames blue with yellow edges,' said Thomas.

'My favourite colour's red,' said Daniel, 'so I'm going to have red windows with green edges.'

They were so happy and excited that they didn't notice that not all the paint was finishing up on the greenhouse. But then Thomas caught sight of himself in a window pane.

'Hey, Dan, look! I'm the Terrible Monster with Orange Hair!'

Then Daniel peered at himself in the glass. His face was covered with paint spots.

'I'm the Green-Spotted Monster,' he giggled.

At that moment they heard steps coming down the path. Suddenly the footsteps stopped. Daniel's mother let out a scream and nearly dropped the tray she was carrying. 'Danny, what on earth have you been doing?' she cried.

From A Treasury of Stories for Five Year Olds *by Nancy Blishen (extract slightly abridged)*

© Letts Educational 1998   **See *Letts Literacy Activity Book 2 Term 1* page 10**

Teaching opportunities at:

TEXT Level
Reading comprehension

1 Look at the picture and ask the children to describe what they can see. Ask them to predict what they think the story is going to be about. *(Answers will depend on the children's interpretation.)*

2 Read the story to the class. Then ask the children to retell it in their own words, without reference to the text. Compare their versions with the original text and discuss any major differences, omissions or additions. Discuss the fact that before stories were written down they were always passed on orally.

3 Go through the story a step at a time and list on the board the different incidents in the passage as they occur. *(Daniel has an idea they paint the greenhouse – Thomas agrees – they find some paint in the cellar – they paint greenhouse different colours – they get covered with paint themselves – Daniel's mum comes out carrying a tray – she sees the boys and shrieks.)* Write each incident on a separate piece of paper, jumble them up and ask the children to re-sequence them correctly. Emphasise the time and sequential relationships in the events.

4 Ask some 'What happened when …' questions based on the events.

5 Do the children think that Daniel and Thomas were deliberately naughty or just thoughtless?

Writing comprehension

1 Ask the children how they think the story might continue. Brainstorm ideas together as a class, encouraging a range of possibilities. Ask the children to choose whichever ending they prefer and to continue the story in their own words.

2 Discuss the children's own experiences of escapades with friends and getting into trouble, then ask them to write an account of one of these.

SENTENCE Level
Grammatical awareness

1 Read the passage again. Leave out some of the adjectives as you do so. Ask the children what difference this makes. Discuss the words that have been omitted and their function. *(Answers will depend on the passage chosen.)* Ask the children to suggest alternative adjectives that could go in each place and consider what changes in meaning occur as a result.

2 This idea could be extended by supplying children with written sentences in which adjectives have been left out and asking them to suggest suitable words to go in the gaps.

3 Similarly, you might give the children any noun, such as 'house' and ask them to suggest ways of describing it, like 'old', 'new', 'big', 'empty', etc.

Sentence construction and punctuation

1 Read the passage again. Point out and discuss the function of the various punctuation marks it contains. *(Apostrophes for contraction and possession, dashes as strong commas, commas for pauses, speech marks, hyphens, exclamation marks for emphasis, question marks and full stops.)* Explain how each of them gives a signal to the reader and affects meaning and expression.

2 Draw attention to the use of capitals letters at the beginning of sentences and for proper nouns (people's names, places, etc.) in the passage. Also note how capitals are used for emphasis in 'GREAT'. Encourage the children to use capitals appropriately in their own writing.

WORD Level
Spelling

1 Use the word 'start' to focus on the phoneme 'ar' in words. Ask the children to suggest other words containing 'ar' and to look for other words in books.

2 Contrast the word 'tray' and 'paint'. Ask the children which letters, or phonemes, make the same sound. Think of, and list, other words containing each phoneme. Draw attention to the fact that 'ai' usually comes within a word, whereas 'ay' usually comes at the end of a word. Extend this by considering 'a_e' words, e.g. 'made'.

3 Look at the word 'now' and 'row' in the passage. Discuss how the 'ow' phoneme can have two different sounds. Think of other words for each category, such as 'cow' or 'grow'. Focus further on the 'ow' phoneme by looking again at 'now'. Find the word 'house' in the text (in 'greenhouse'). Notice that 'ou' and 'ow' sound the same. Look for and list other 'ou' words in other reading books. Note that 'colour' and 'you' in the passage don't follow this pattern!

Vocabulary extension

1 Look for and discuss any unfamiliar words in the text, for instance, 'cellar'.

2 List the words 'greenhouse', 'rainbow' and 'footsteps' on the board. Point out that each word is made up of two shorter words. Can the children think of any others like this? You might like to encourage them by suggesting 'toothbrush', 'tablecloth', 'snowflake', etc.

Related texts

'Stories for Five Year Olds' ed. by Sara and Stephen Corrin

'Stories for Six Year Olds' ed. by Sara and Stephen Corrin

'Playtime Stories' by Joyce Donaghue

A Recipe for Gingerbread Men

About the text

Recipes are a good way of introducing children to instructional writing – as well as having a practical outcome! This recipe for gingerbread men could most effectively be tried out as part of the reading activity.

Teaching opportunities at:

TEXT Level
Reading comprehension

1 Look at the title and the picture. Ask the children to retell, in their own words, the well-known traditional story in which the old woman and old man bake a gingerbread biscuit. The gingerbread man comes to life and runs away. The poem has the recurring refrain: 'Run, run as fast as you can. You can't catch me, I'm the gingerbread man'.

2 Now ask the children to look at the way the text is set out and to predict what sort of a text it is going to be. A quick glance at the headings and pictures should give enough clues. *(It is an instructional text. It is entitled 'a recipe', it contains a 'What you need' section, a list of ingredients and numbered step-by-step instructions.)*

3 Read the three sections one at a time. Use phonological, contextual, grammatical and graphic knowledge to work out, predict and check the meanings of unfamiliar words and to make sense of what they read.

4 Discuss why the 'What you need' section comes first. *(To ensure one is well-prepared to continue uninterrupted through the instructions.)*

5 Ask the children to suggest what 'ingredients' and 'equipment' mean.

6 Read and discuss the ingredients. Ask the children why it is necessary to be careful when gathering or weighing each ingredient. Discuss each individual ingredient. Talk about the different ways of measuring mentioned in the text, focusing on measures of weight. *('Teaspoons', 'grams', and 'a pinch'.)* If appropriate, you might like to point out that temperature is a form of measure. *('Gas Mark 3 (168°C/335°F)'.)*

7 Follow the same procedure for the 'equipment' section.

8 Why are the steps in the 'What to do' section numbered? How does this help? *(It makes it easy to follow the instructions in order, and in easily digestible chunks.)* Read through them and draw attention to the direct, concise language used.

Key Stage 1
Literacy Poster Pack 2
Letts EDUCATIONAL

A Recipe for Gingerbread Men
You will need:

INGREDIENTS
3 teaspoons of golden syrup
3 teaspoons of ground ginger
250g self-raising flour
50g margarine
100g caster sugar
currants
glacé cherries
a pinch of salt

EQUIPMENT
a greased baking tray
a sieve
a mixing bowl
a wooden spoon
a saucepan

What to do:
1 Sieve together the ginger, salt and flour into the mixing bowl.
2 Melt together the margarine, syrup and sugar in the saucepan.
3 Stir in the dry ingredients and leave the mixture until it is cool.
4 Shape the mixture into 'men' and lay them on the greased baking tray.
5 Press in currant 'eyes and buttons' and a sliced cherry 'mouth'.
6 Place in a hot oven at Gas Mark 3 (168°C/335°F) for a quarter of an hour.

© Letts Educational 1998   See *Letts Literacy Activity Book 2 Term 1* page 12

9 Ask the children if they ever help at home with cooking. What sort of things do they make? Do they use recipes? Discuss the potential dangers and hazards of working in the kitchen, and the need for adult supervision.

Writing comprehension

1 As a class, discuss some familiar process, like brushing teeth or having a bath. Ask one child to suggest the instructions that might make the task easy and write them on the board. As a class study them to see how they can be improved or if any others need adding. Finally, number them in order.

2 Copy out the instructions, without the numbers, and cut them up into individual sentences. Ask the children to re-sequence them correctly.

3 Ask the children to write instructions for playing a simple game, perhaps noughts and crosses.

SENTENCE Level
Grammatical awareness

1 When writing instructions (see Writing comprehension), encourage the children to use appropriate linking words and phrases to help structure them, for instance, 'after', 'first', 'before', 'next', 'then', 'after a while', etc.

Sentence construction and punctuation

1 When writing instructions (see Writing comprehension), these could be presented in the form of a simple flow diagram, with arrows linking each step in order.

WORD Level
Spelling

1 The 'ingredients' of all words are vowels and consonants. Choose some of the words from the text and write them on the board, missing out all the vowels. Ask the children to find the words in the text and fill in the missing letters. Draw attention to the fact that nearly every word must contain at least one vowel. If appropriate, make sure the children appreciate that there are very few exceptions to this rule.

2 Look for the words containing the long vowel phonemes 'ea' and 'oo' in the text. ('ea': 'gingerbread', 'teaspoon', 'greased', 'leave'; 'oo': teaspoon, 'wooden', 'spoon', 'cool'.) Ask the children to think of some other words containing the same phonemes.

3 Select some of the longer words from the text, such as 'together', and ask the children to see how many smaller words they can find hiding in each word. Use letters that run consecutively only, and not anagrams. (In this case, 'to', 'get', 'her' and 'the'.)

Vocabulary extension

1 Try classifying the ingredients listed, perhaps into sweet or sour, wet or dry. Then classify each by the way they are measured. Think of some other ingredients that could go in each category.

2 Make a list of cooking utensils and kitchen tools. What is each used for?

Related texts

'Sugar and Spice: Wickedly Delicious Cookies and Candies for Junior Chefs' by Nicola Fowler

'Crafty Ideas with Cookery' by Melanie Rice

'Brownie Cook Book' by Myra Street

'Busy Little Cook' by Judy Bastyra

The Sick Young Dragon

About the text

This delightful poem tells the story of the young dragon who is ill in bed – he can't seem to get his fire to burn or blow flames! However, after a visit from the doctor, he's soon put right and is sneezing sparks and setting light to his bedclothes.

Key Stage 1
Literacy Poster Pack 2

Letts EDUCATIONAL

The Sick Young Dragon

'What can I do?' young dragon cried.
'Although I've simply tried and tried,
It doesn't matter how hard I blow,
I cannot get my fire to go!'

'Open your mouth!' his mother said.
'It's no wonder! Your throat's not red.
Your scales are cold. You must be ill.
I think you must have caught a chill.'

The doctor came. He looked and said,
'You'll need a day or two in bed.
Your temperature's down. No doubt
That's the reason your fire's gone out.

'Just drink this petrol. Chew these nails.
They'll help you to warm up your scales.
Just take it easy. Watch TV,
You'll soon be right as rain, you'll see.'

Young dragon did as he was told
And soon his scales stopped feeling cold.
He sneezed some sparks. His face
    glowed bright.
He coughed and set the sheets alight.

'Oh dear!' he cried. 'I've burnt the bed!'
'It doesn't matter,' his mother said.
'Those sheets were old. Go out and play.
Just watch where you breathe your
    fire today!'

From A Very First Poetry Book by John Foster

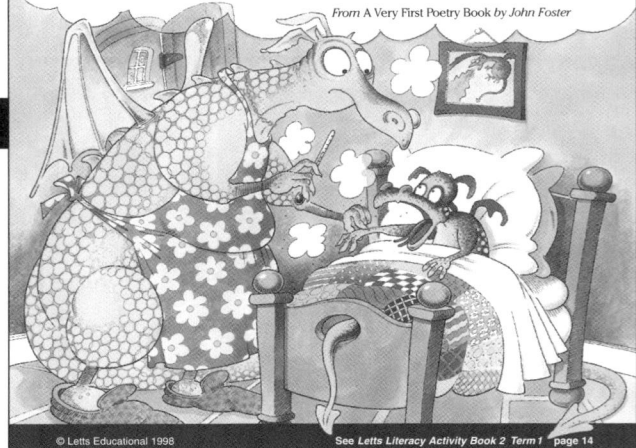

© Letts Educational 1998   See *Letts Literacy Activity Book 2 Term 1* page 14

Teaching opportunities at:

TEXT Level
Reading comprehension

1 Look at the picture and the title and ask the children what they think the poem is going to be about. Encourage them to volunteer what sort of things a dragon usually does. Then talk about how it feels to be under the weather and confined to bed. What illnesses have they had? Have they ever been visited by a doctor? Ask the children to talk about their anecdotal experiences of being sick.

2 Read the poem to and with the class, taking note of who is talking. Use different voices for the dragon, his mother and the doctor.

3 Use a variety of cues to decode any difficult or unfamiliar words, like 'temperature'.

4 Ask some 'What happened when ...' questions based on the text.

5 Discuss the way the poem is set out. Use the term verses. *(It is set out in six verses and rhyming couplets.)* Then draw attention to the fact that each pair of words rhyme. Identify the pairs of rhyming words. ('Cried/tried', 'blow/go', 'said/read', 'ill/chill', 'said/bed', 'doubt/out', 'nails/scales', 'TV/see', 'told/cold', 'bright/alight', 'bed/said', 'play/today'.)

6 Encourage the children to read the poem several times to each other, and to collect other poems about illness or dragons and to compare them.

Writing comprehension

1 Ask the children to write personal accounts of when they were ill. What was the problem? How did they feel? Where were they? What happened? How did they get better? (This might need to be treated with sensitivity.)

2 Think of other things that could happen to the young dragon, e.g. his first day at dragon school, he gets lost, he goes on holiday, etc. As a class, work on a class poem around one of these themes.

SENTENCE Level
Grammatical awareness

1 Ask the children to retell the story in their own words. Write a structure on the board for them to work within on the lines of: 'First… Then… So… Then… After a while…', etc.

Sentence construction and punctuation

1 Read the poem again with the children. Point out any punctuation marks when you come to them and discuss their importance and functions. *(Speech marks, question marks, full stops, apostrophes for contraction and possession, commas for pauses and exclamation marks.)*

2 Draw attention to the use of punctuation in class work and encourage the children to check their own work for correct punctuation.

WORD Level
Spelling

1 Use some words from the poem to do some work on pluralising regular nouns with 's'. Take the words 'scale', 'nail', 'spark' and 'sheet'. Write two columns on the board, one headed 'one' the other headed 'two'. Say and write 'One scale but two scales. One nail but two nails', and so on. Draw attention to how each word is suffixed in the plural. Add other words to the list for the children to pluralise, like 'day', 'bed', 'dragon', 'doctor', 'bag', 'face', 'friend', etc.

2 Use some words from the poem to do some work on suffixing regular verbs in the past tense with '-ed'. Use the verbs 'look', 'glow' and 'cough'. Find these verbs in the text and notice how they have been suffixed. *('Look + ed' to make 'looked'.)* Give the children some more regular verbs to suffix in the same way, like 'jump', 'walk', 'turn', 'open', 'knock', 'shout', 'cook', etc.

Vocabulary extension

1 As a class, brainstorm and list as many words as possible to do with being ill, such as 'cough', 'sneeze', 'ill', 'sick', 'temperature', 'hospital', 'doctor', and so on.

2 Have fun seeing how many small words can be spotted 'hiding' in some of the longer words like 'temperature'. Use letters that run consecutively only, and not anagrams. *('Temper', 'rat' and 'at'.)*

Related texts

Some titles compiled by John Foster:
'A Red Poetry Paintbox'
'A Blue Poetry Paintbox'
'Twinkle, Twinkle Chocolate Bar'

Other poetry books:
' "Stand Back," Said the Elephant, "I'm Going to Sneeze" ' by Patricia Thomas and Wallace Tripp
'Quentin Blake's Book of Nonsense Verse' ed. Quentin Blake.

The Snowy Day

About the text

'One winter morning Peter woke up and looked out of the window. Snow had fallen during the night.' This passage tells of Peter's experiences of the snow.

Teaching opportunities at:

TEXT Level
Reading comprehension

1 Before reading the text, look at the title and picture. Encourage the children to talk about their experiences of snow. How do they feel when they look out of the window and see it falling? How do they dress when they go out in it? What sort of things do they do? Have they ever built a snowman? How? Have they ever had a snowball fight? Have they ever been on a sledge? How does everything look when covered in snow? Elicit from them unpleasant, as well as pleasant, experiences.

2 Read the story to the class. Encourage them to use and apply their word level skills and a variety of cues to unlock the meaning of any difficult words, like 'breakfast' and as an aid to making sense of what is read.

3 After reading, ask a range of 'Why' questions, encouraging the children to identify reasons for events in the story, for instance, 'Why didn't Peter play with the big boys?'

4 Ask a range of 'What happened when …' questions to help the children understand time and sequential relationships in the story. Ask questions like 'What happened when he smacked the tree with a stick?'

5 Draw attention to the writer's use of noise words in the text. *('Crunch', 'smacking' and 'plop'.)* Ask the children to think of and suggest other 'noise' words.

6 Ask the children to retell the story in their own words, without reference to the text. Compare their versions with the original and discuss any major differences.

Writing comprehension

1 The story ends with Peter calling for his friend and them going out to play in the snow. Discuss the sorts of adventures they might have had. Write words, phrases and sentences on the board as reminders. Ask the children to continue the story.

2 Many children will have seen or read the Raymond Briggs' book 'The Snowman' about the snowman who comes to life. Encourage the class to imagine the snowman they built does the same, and to make up a story of some of the things they do together.

Key Stage 1
Literacy Poster Pack 2
Letts EDUCATIONAL

The Snowy Day

One winter morning Peter woke up and looked out of the window. Snow had fallen during the night. It covered everything as far as he could see.

After breakfast he put on his snowsuit and ran outside. The snow was piled up very high along the street to make a path for walking.

Crunch, crunch, crunch, his feet sank into the snow. He dragged his feet s-l-o-w-l-y to make tracks. And he found something sticking out of the snow that made a new track. It was a stick – a stick that was just right for smacking a snow-covered tree. Down fell the snow – plop! – on top of Peter's head.

He thought it would be fun to join the big boys in their snowball fight, but he knew he wasn't old enough – not yet. So he made a smiling snowman, and he made angels. He pretended he was a mountain climber. He climbed up a great tall, heaping mountain of snow – and slid all the way down.

He picked up a handful of snow – and another, and still another. He packed it round and firm and put the snowball in his pocket for tomorrow. Then he went into his warm house.

He told his mother all about his adventures while she took off his wet socks. And he thought, and thought, and thought about them.

Before he got into bed he looked in his pocket. His pocket was empty. The snowball wasn't there. He felt very sad.

While he slept, he dreamed that the sun had melted all the snow away.

But when he woke up his dream was gone. The snow was still everywhere. New snow was falling!

After breakfast he called for his friend from across the hall, and they went out together in the deep, deep snow.

From The Snowy Day by Ezra Jack Keats

© Letts Educational 1998   See *Letts Literacy Activity Book 2* Term 1   page 16

SENTENCE Level
Grammatical awareness

1 Find some examples of the use of the conjunction 'and' in the story. *(There are many possible examples.)* Discuss how it can join two shorter sentences and make one long sentence, for example, 'One winter morning Peter woke up and looked out of the window' can be broken into 'One winter morning Peter woke up. He looked out of the window'.

2 Try giving the children pairs of sentences for them to join in this way, noting any changes needed to do so.

3 In the text, find other examples of words that link sentences together. *('After', 'but', 'then', 'before' and 'while'.)*

Sentence construction and punctuation

1 Use the text to reinforce understanding of the use of capital letters for people's names and at the beginning of sentences. Provide the children with some sentences containing proper nouns which have been incorrectly punctuated, for them to rewrite correctly.

2 Draw attention to the use of exclamation marks in the text and the effect they have on intonation and expression. Notice, too, the way of writing the word 's-l-o-w-l-y'. Discuss why it is written like this. *(To turn the word in to the action and make it clear how it should be spoken.)*

WORD Level
Spelling

1 Use some words from the text to do some work on pluralising regular nouns with 's'. Draw attention to how words such as 'angel' and 'boy' are suffixed in the plural. Add other words to the list for children to pluralise.

2 Look for verbs in the story ending in '-ing' or '-ed', such as 'walking'. Point out how these consist of a root word plus the suffix. *('Walk + ing'.)* Take some more verbs from the story to which '-ing' or '-ed' may be added without changing the root word. *('Stick', 'smack', 'heap', 'fall'; 'look', 'cover', 'pretend', 'climb', 'pick', 'pack', 'dream', 'melt', 'call'.)* Ask the children to make these into '-ing' and '-ed' words.

Vocabulary extension

1 Link this to Writing comprehension. Encourage the children to offer as many 'snow-related' words as possible. Take the opportunity to develop spelling skills during this session. As an extra activity, the words could be sorted into alphabetical order according to their first letters.

Related texts

Other titles by Ezra Jack Keats:

'Hi Cat'

'A Letter to Amy'

'Maggie and the Pirate'

'Peter's Chair'

Stories with snow themes:

'The Snowman' by Raymond Briggs

'The Snow Storm' by Adam Coleman

'Bluff and Bran and the Snowdrift' by Meg Rutherford

'The Snow Child' by Debi Gliori

Trees

About the text

Trees are all round us – but how often do children stop and think about them? This poem encourages children to reflect on them in a number of different ways.

Teaching opportunities at:

TEXT Level
Reading comprehension

1 Before reading, ask the children to volunteer anything they know about trees – types of trees, why they are important, what wood is used for, what animals live in them, and so on.

2 Read the poem to the class. Elicit the children's immediate response to it. Did they enjoy it? Why? Why not?

3 Refer to the acknowledgement and ask the children who wrote the poem. *(Harry Behn.)* How did the poet feel about trees? Notice the first and last lines. *(He thinks trees are the kindest thing he knows.)*

4 Ask the children to list some of the positive things the poet says about trees. *(They provide shade, they give fruit, they provide wood and they 'hum a drowsy lullaby'.)*

5 Discuss some of the harder to understand verses with the children, in particular, the last two verses.

6 Draw attention to the fact that the poem is written in eight verses, each containing two lines, and that each pair of lines rhyme.

Key Stage 1
Literacy Poster Pack 2 — *Letts* EDUCATIONAL

Trees

Trees are the kindest things I know,
They do no harm, they simply grow

And spread a shade for sleepy cows,
And gather birds among their boughs.

They give us fruit in leaves above,
And wood to make our houses of,

And leaves to burn on Halloween
And in the Spring new buds of green.

They are the first when day's begun
To touch the beams of morning sun,

They are the last to hold the light
When evening changes into night,

And when the moon floats on the sky
They hum a drowsy lullaby

Of sleepy children long ago...
Trees are the kindest things I know.

From Earthways by Harry Behn

© Letts Educational 1998   See *Letts Literacy Activity Book 2* Term 1   page 18

Writing comprehension

1 The poet has written from the point of view of someone who likes trees. Encourage the children to think of some bad points about trees, perhaps that they block out the light, they suck the ground dry, they 'attract' lightning, and they harbour lots of creepy crawlies. Try writing a class anti-tree poem!

2 If appropriate, share some of the following thoughts about trees and ask the children to write some factual sentences about them. Trees play a vital part of life on earth. Without them no animals or humans could survive. They provide a basic source of food and nourishment. Trees are the largest of plants and live the longest of them all. A tree is made up of a trunk (the stem), branches and twigs (the crown), and leaves which absorb sunlight which is necessary for all plant growth. A tree also has flowers, fruit sap and roots. The age of a tree can be calculated from the trunk. Each year a new growth ring is added and, when felled, the rings can be counted. The roots of a tree are very important. They serve three functions. They hold the tree in the ground; they are the main source of water gathering for the tree; and they search for nutrients in the soil.

SENTENCE Level
Grammatical awareness

1 Try reading the poem and leaving gaps where the verbs are, to draw attention to their function. Do this without giving children access to the original and ask them to suggest appropriate words for each gap. *(Answers will depend on the section chosen.)*

Sentence construction and punctuation

1 Punctuation plays an important part in helping make sense of poetry. In this poem, draw attention to the use of commas which require the reader to pause. Note how they often occur at the end of lines. Draw attention to those lines which do not end in a comma (or a full stop) indicating that the reader should read on without pausing.

WORD Level
Spelling

1 Try 'growing' some new words from words in the poem. Use these as starters and develop others from words in the poem: change the 'tr' in 'tree' to 'b', 's', 'fr', 'gl' and 'thr'. *('Bee', 'see', 'free', 'glee' and 'three'.)* Change the 'sh' in 'shade' to 'f', 'm', 'w' and 'bl'. *('Fade', 'made', 'wade', and 'blade'.)* Change the 'spr' of 'spread' to 'h', 'd', 'l', 'br' and 'dr'. *('Head', 'dead', 'lead', 'bread' and 'dread'.)* Change the 'spr' of 'spring' into 'k', 'r', 's', 'w', 'br' and 'fl'. *('King', 'ring', 'sing', 'wing', 'bring' and 'fling'.)*

Vocabulary extension

1 Draw a large outline picture of a tree and fill it with any tree-related vocabulary the children can come up with. If appropriate, link this with the suggested task in Writing comprehension, points 1 and 2.

Related texts

Some conservation books which look at the environment:

'Brother Eagle, Sister Sky' by Chief Seattle and illustrated by Susan Jeffers

Other titles about trees:

'The Living Tree' by Nigel Hester

'A First Guide to Trees' by Simon Perry

'The Usborne Nature Trail Book of Trees and Leaves' by Ingrid Selberg

'Trees' by Theresa Greenaway

The School Visit

About the text

The poster consists of a plan of the London Wildlife Centre and is useful for discussing features of plans and giving directions and instructions.

Teaching opportunities at:

TEXT Level
Reading comprehension

1 Look at the poster together as a class. Ask the children how it is possible to tell what it is a plan of. *(The children's speech indicates it is a play of the London Wildlife Centre.)*

2 Discuss what a plan is. *(It is a large-scale drawing or map, looking down on an area from above.)* Ask the children to imagine they are in a tall building or hot air balloon looking down on the centre. The plan shows what they would see.

3 Draw attention to the numbers on the plan. Discuss why they are there. How would they help a visitor? *(They keep the picture of the plan 'clean' and act as quick reference for the key.)*

4 Find the key on the plan. Explain the purpose of it and relate some of the numbers on the plan to it, to discover what they represent. Ask the children to suggest reasons why a key is important. Why might it be called a 'key'? *(It 'unlocks' the number code.)*

5 Describe some of the places in riddle form and ask the children to suggest where you are in the Centre. For example, 'I can hear a buzzing sound nearby. A lot of yellow and black flying insects are coming and going from this. Where am I?'

6 Ask some directional or positional questions such as, 'What is nearest the Visitors' Centre?' 'If I sit on the bench in the picnic area, what is straight ahead of me?' *(The woodland corner is nearest, though the children might suggest the tree nursery/raised seed beds. The big pond is straight ahead.)*

Writing comprehension

1 Ask the children to make up some more 'riddle-type' questions (as in Reading comprehension, point 5).

2 Encourage the children to write some simple directions for getting to different places in your school, starting from different points, such as from the classroom, from the hall, etc.

SENTENCE Level
Grammatical awareness

1 Go through the items on the key one at a time. Where they are unfamiliar words or are difficult to decode, look at what each represents as a cue to the meaning of the word.

Sentence construction and punctuation

1 Make a simple plan of something familiar to the children, like the classroom or playground. Do this as a class exercise and discuss what would need to go on it, where and how it would be represented. Design a key to go with it. Use the plan on the poster as a model.

2 Use the plan you made without the key. Ask the children to make labels for various parts of the plan and draw arrows from each label to the aspect it refers to.

WORD Level
Spelling

1 Ask the children to write some of the words from the key in their books and to underline, circle or colour the vowels in each. (*Answers will depend on the words chosen.*)

2 Ask the children to look for words with the following smaller words 'hiding' in them: 'post', 'corn', 'wild', 'nurse', 'edge', 'eat', 'are', 'on', 'low', 'or', 'ring', and 'itch'. (*'Post': 'compost'; 'corn': 'corner'; 'wild': 'wildlife', 'wildflower'; 'nurse': 'nursery'; 'edge': 'hedgerow'; 'eat': 'seating'; 'are': 'area'; 'on': 'London', 'only', 'pond', 'container'; 'low': 'follow', 'wildflower', 'flower'; 'or': 'corner', 'border', 'short', 'visitors'; 'ring': 'spring'; 'itch': 'ditch'.*)

Vocabulary extension

1 List places of special interest nearby that children have visited or would like to visit. Draw attention to the use of capital letters at the beginning of names of special places.

Related texts

'Maps and Mapping' by Barbara Taylor

'Maps and Journeys' by Kate Petty

'Be Your Own Map Expert' by Barbara Taylor

'Mapstart' by Simon Catling

The Birthday Present

About the text

A small girl does not know what to get her mum for a birthday present, so she asks Mr Rabbit for his advice. This extract by Charlotte Zolotow revolves around gifts of different colours.

Key Stage 1
Literacy Poster Pack 2

Letts EDUCATIONAL

The Birthday Present

A little girl asks a rabbit for some advice on what she could give her mother as a present for her birthday.

'What is red?' asked the little girl.
'Well,' said Mr Rabbit, 'there's red underwear.'
'No,' said the little girl, 'I can't give her that.'
'There are red roofs,' said Mr Rabbit.
'No, we have a red roof,' said the little girl. 'I don't want to give her that.'
'There are red birds,' said Mr Rabbit, 'red cardinals.'
'No,' said the little girl, 'she likes birds in trees.'
'There are red fire engines,' said Mr Rabbit.

'No,' said the little girl, 'she doesn't like fire engines.'
'Well,' said Mr Rabbit, 'there are apples.'
'Good,' said the little girl. 'That's good. She likes apples. But I need something else.'
'What else does she like?' said Mr Rabbit.
'Well, she likes yellow,' said the little girl.
'Well,' said Mr Rabbit, 'there are yellow taxicabs.'
'I'm sure she doesn't want a taxicab,' said the little girl.
'The sun is yellow,' said Mr Rabbit.
'I can't give her the sun,' the little girl said, 'though I would if I could.'
'A canary bird is yellow,' said Mr Rabbit.
'She likes birds in trees,' said the little girl.
'That's right, you told me,' said Mr Rabbit.
'Well, butter is yellow. Does she like butter?'
'We have butter,' said the little girl.
'Bananas are yellow,' said Mr Rabbit.
'Oh, good. That's good,' said the little girl. 'She likes bananas. I need something else, though.'

From Mr Rabbit and the Lovely Present *by Charlotte Zolotow (slightly adapted)*

© Letts Educational 1998   See *Letts Literacy Activity Book 2* Term 1 page 22

Teaching opportunities at:

TEXT Level
Reading comprehension

1 Discuss how the title, the picture and the introductory sentence give clues as to what the story might be about. *(The title is 'The Birthday Present', and the introduction explains the situation.)*

2 Talk about birthdays. Discuss the anticipation and the waiting for birthdays to come around as they near. Ask the class to discuss why we have birthdays and why people give each other presents.

3 Read the story to the class, changing the voice intonation each time either the rabbit or the girl speaks.

4 Ask the children how, when they read the story they know each time a different person speaks. *(The speech alternates between the girl and the rabbit and they are named nearly every time.)*

5 Why might the girl have asked the rabbit's advice? What was the relationship between the girl and the rabbit? *(For instance, she clearly sees the rabbit as a friend and someone who is wise – someone who's advice she can seek and who's advice she can rely upon.)*

6 Think of some words that might be used to describe the rabbit, like 'helpful', 'friendly', 'wise', etc.

7 Where did their conversation take place? Does it say? Is it possible to guess? Give reasons. Does the picture give any clues? If not, suggest it was probably in the woods.

8 Ask the children what they would give a specific grown-up for a present (mother, father, brother, sister, aunt, etc.). Who would they ask for advice if they didn't know what to get? How do people know what to choose each other for presents?

Writing comprehension

1 Ask the children to imagine they had been sent a particular present by an aunt or uncle. Encourage them to write a thank-you letter.

2 Ask them to write letters to Father Christmas, listing at least four or five things they would like. Encourage them to punctuate their letters correctly, especially with commas separating items on their lists.

SENTENCE Level
Grammatical awareness

1 Ask the children to rewrite the conversation about one of the colours as a series of sentences, using appropriate sequencing words to link the sentences together. *(For example, 'First of all the girl asked Mr Rabbit what was red. When he suggested underwear the little girl said that she could not give her mum that. Then…')*

Sentence construction and punctuation

1 Read the passage again. Point out the use of speech marks denoting when a person begins and finishes speaking. Pay special attention to question marks at the end of questions asked, too.

WORD Level
Spelling

1 Ask the children to find all the words containing double consonants in the passage. *('Little', 'rabbit' 'well', 'apples', 'yellow' and 'butter'.)* Suggest they list other words they can think of containing each of the double consonants they have found. *(The consonants being 'tt', 'bb', 'll', 'pp', 'tt'.)*

2 Ask the children to find all the words containing double vowels in the passage. *('Trees', 'need', 'roof' and 'good'.)* Suggest they list other words they can think of containing each of the double vowels they have found. *(The vowels being 'ee', 'oo'.)*

3 Hold a 'high frequency word' hunt. Give the children a selection of High Frequency Words from pages 74–75 and ask them to see how many of these they can find in the passage.

Vocabulary extension

1 Brainstorm and list animals that live in woods, that live in jungles or that live in the desert. Write the animals' names down under different headings to emphasise the different 'sets' or 'classes' of animals.

Related texts

Other titles by Charlotte Zolotow:
'The Sky Was Blue'
'Wish You Were Here'

Books with presents as a theme:
'Harvey Slumfenberger's Christmas Present' by John Burningham

'Santa Claus Takes Off' by Victor and Glenys Ambrus

Helping Hedgehogs Hibernate

About the text

The poster includes step-by-step instructions for making a hibernation nest for hedgehogs.

Teaching opportunities at:

TEXT Level
Reading comprehension

1 Read the title and introduction to the class. Discuss the children's experiences of hedgehogs, if any, and what knowledge they have of them. Discuss the word 'hibernate' in the context of the sentence. If appropriate, also show children how to look the word up in a dictionary to check its meaning. Discuss how a hibernation nest could be useful for hedgehogs during the winter.

2 Read the 'What you do' section and each of the steps in the process. Why are they numbered? Are they clear?

3 Discuss any unfamiliar words in the instructions. Encourage children to work out their meanings using any cues available. *(Answers will depend on the section chosen.)* Try replacing some of these words with synonyms, for example, instead of using 'insert', you might try 'put in', etc.

4 Notice the direct language used in the instructions. Discuss the fact that instructions are usually written like commands or orders, telling you what to do, but that the word 'you' is not used. *('(You) insert the large plastic entrance pipe', etc.)* You might like to point out that the use of verbs in this way is called the 'imperative'.

5 Cover up the 'What you do' section and ask the children to try to explain the process in their own words, using appropriate linking words to emphasise the sequence of actions.

Key Stage 1
Literacy Poster Pack 2
Letts EDUCATIONAL

Helping Hedgehogs Hibernate
In Winter, we hibernate. We like to find somewhere dry and warm to shelter, so we can sleep peacefully. A hibernation nest will provide us with a safe, cosy shelter all winter.

What you do:

Step 1
Put a thick layer of dry grass and leaves on the floor of the box.

Step 2
Stand the box on two bricks in a sheltered spot.

Step 3
Cut a hole in one side of the box near the bottom.

Step 4
Insert the large plastic entrance pipe.

Step 5
Cut a smaller hole in the middle of the side of the box.

Step 6
Insert the ventilation pipe.

Step 7
Cover the box with a mixture of dry soil and dead leaves.

Step 8
Place a polythene sheet over the shelter.

Step 9
Put some heavy stones on the sheet so it will not blow away.

Step 10
Make sure the entrance and ventilation pipe is kept clear (as shown in the diagram).

© Letts Educational 1998   See *Letts Literacy Activity Book 2 Term 1*   page 24

Writing comprehension

1 Apply the same thinking to encouraging children to write an explanation of how to make something simple. You might link this with Technology, as in making a glove puppet from an old sock. Suggest the children use the poster layout as a model.

SENTENCE Level
Grammatical awareness

1 Read the 'What you do' section again, leaving out the verbs. (Do not allow children access to the poster!) Ask them to suggest an appropriate word for each missing verb. *(The children will come up with many different suggestions.)* Point out that these words are all important in telling you what to do – they are 'doing' words.

Sentence construction and punctuation

1 When working on the 'Writing comprehension' activity, encourage the children to use a labelled diagram, with arrows.

2 Reproduce the 'What you do' section (leaving out the numbering for the steps) in the incorrect order. Ask the children to cut out each step and sequence them correctly. These could be stuck in their books in the form of a flow diagram, with each step being joined with an arrow to the next to emphasise the sequential nature of the process.

WORD Level
Spelling

1 Use the text for a 'letter pattern' hunt. Give the children a number of letter patterns, e.g. 'ck', 'ss', 'sh', 'er', etc., and ask them to find as many words as possible in the text containing each. *('ck': 'thick', 'brick'; 'ss': 'grass'; 'sh': 'sheltered', 'sheet', 'shelter', 'shown'; 'er': 'hibernate', 'winter', 'somewhere', 'shelter', 'hibernation', 'layer', 'sheltered', 'insert', 'smaller', 'cover', 'over'.)* Ask them to think of at least one more word containing each letter pattern, and to use some of the words in their own made-up sentences.

Vocabulary extension

1 Give children a list of animals and their habitats. Ask them to match each animal and its home and to write a sentence for each, for example, 'A rabbit lives in a burrow'.

Related texts

'The Blue Peter Book of Things to Make' by Margaret Parnell

'Crafty Ideas for Presents' by Myrna Daitz

'A First Guide Book to Making Models' by Diana Craig

'My Craft Book' by Cheryl Owen

'The Simply Wonderful Craft Book' by Lois Rock

Some hedgehog/wildlife titles:

'Hedgehogs' by Joanne Jessop

'Wildfire Through the Year' by Andrew Cleave

Enough for Two?

About the text

The only thing Anwar can think of is water. He is parched. When he reaches the well, a pitifully thin dog looks at him hopefully. What should he do? Get water for himself or for the dog?

Teaching opportunities at:

TEXT Level
Reading comprehension

1 Look at the picture and discuss with the children what can be learned from it, for example, where it is set, the things that can be seen, any characters (and how they are dressed) and animals in the picture. What is the boy doing? Ask the children to suggest why this might be. *(The scene is dry and dusty, with no landscape features. There is only the well. Anwar, the boy, looks thin, as does the dog. The boy is giving the dog some water from his boot.)*

2 Read the story to the class. Discuss occasions when the children have felt very thirsty. How easy is it for us to get water? How easy was it for Anwar?

3 Using the description in the story, ask the children to describe what a well is. How do we know it was a deep well? *(There was silence for a second before the stone Anwar dropped hit water.)* Can children think of any other rhymes or stories in which wells are mentioned?

4 Why would the water in the well be cool and not warm? *(It is deep underground and in the dark.)*

5 If Anwar had not used his boot, what other suggestions can the children make for getting water to the dog?

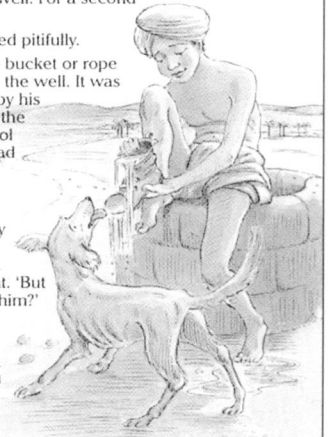

Key Stage 1
Literacy Poster Pack 2

Enough for Two?

The sun was like a burning ball of fire, high in the blue sky. The road was long and dusty. The only thing Anwar could think of was water. He was hot! Very hot! Then, just ahead, he saw a well. 'I expect it will be dry, like the others,' he said to himself.

As he got nearer he saw a skinny dog lying beside it. Anwar could see its bones it was so thin. 'Get out of my way,' Anwar said. He was desperate to get to the well. He picked up a stone and dropped it into the darkness of the well. For a second there was silence and then Plop!

'Water,' cried Anwar. The dog whined pitifully.

The problem was that there was no bucket or rope so Anwar had to climb down inside the well. It was slow going, and he had to cling on by his fingers and toes. At last he reached the bottom. There it was – beautiful, cool water. He poured some over his head and drank great gulps of it, until he felt completely refreshed.

He was just about to make his way out of the well again when suddenly a picture of the poor old dog came into his mind. 'He is just as much in need of a drink as I was,' he thought. 'But how can I carry some water up for him?' Then an idea came into his head.

A few minutes later, when he reached the top of the well, the dog looked up. Anwar smiled. 'Here you are. You must be thirsty. This water is for you,' he said and held out his boot – full of water! The poor old dog's tail wagged and his eyes lit up as if to say, 'Thank you!'

A story from India

© Letts Educational 1998   See *Letts Literacy Activity Book 2 Term 2* page 6

6 Ask the children to discuss how the saying 'All's well that ends well' could be applied to the story.

Writing comprehension

1 Ask the children to rewrite the story in their own words.

2 Turn the story into a fairy tale along the lines of the Frog Prince. Imagine that the dog is really a princess who has been turned into a dog and can only change back if someone performs an act of kindness for her. The children should write the story and make up a suitable fairytale ending.

SENTENCE Level
Grammatical awareness

1 Encourage the children to read the story aloud using intonation and expression appropriate to the grammar and punctuation. Make sure they pay special attention to exclamation marks and to stopping at the end of each sentence appropriately.

2 Encourage the children to reread their own versions of the story to check for grammatical sense and accuracy.

Sentence construction and punctuation

1 Ask the children to identify the speech marks in the text and to explain their purpose. (*The speech marks are used for both the words spoken aloud and silent thoughts.*) Find examples of speech marks in other texts they are reading.

WORD Level
Spelling

1 Discuss the fact that we can break longer words down into smaller parts called syllables. Use the words 'Anwar', 'water', 'dusty' and 'ahead' to demonstrate. Say the words slowly and tap out the beat of each syllable as you do so. Each of the given words consists of two syllables. (*'An/war', 'wa/ter', 'dus/ty' and 'a/head'.*) Try the clapping syllable beats test to check. Ask the children to find at least ten other words in the passage which contain two syllables. Can any children find any three syllable words? (*There are many possible examples.*)

Vocabulary extension

1 Ask the children to supply the names of children in the class which consist of two syllables. Write these in alphabetical order according to the first letter in each.

Related texts

'The Wizard Punchkin: A Folk Tale from India' by Joanna Troughton

'Seasons of Splendour: Tales, Myths and Legends of India' by Madhur Jaffrey

'The Story of Running Water' by Joanna Troughton

'Water' by Paola Jervis (A non-fiction title on water as a natural resource.)

The Story of Milk

About the text

This explanatory text explains the process by which milk gets from the cow to the shops. It is in the form of a picture story with captions, set out as a flow diagram.

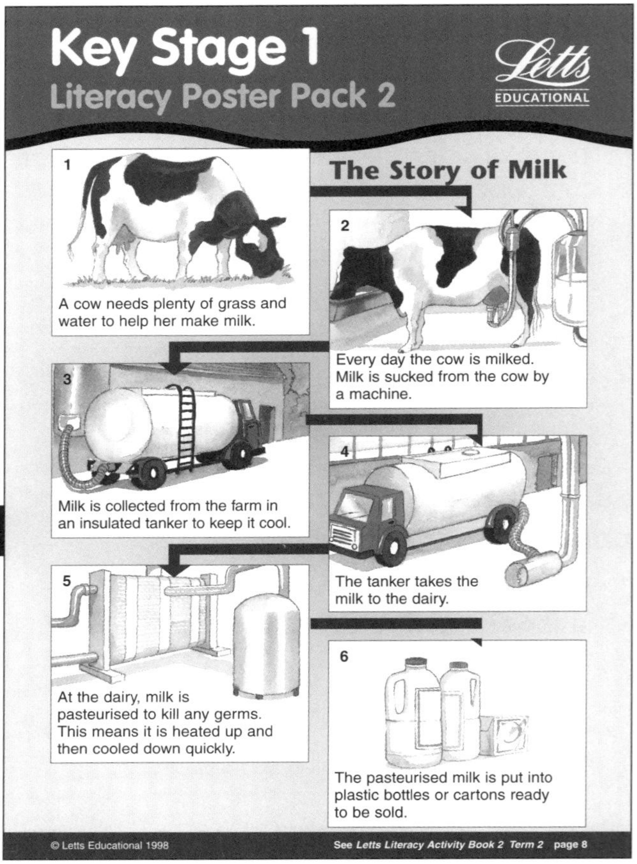

Teaching opportunities at:

TEXT Level
Reading comprehension

1 Look at the title and glance quickly at the pictures. Ask the children what they expect the text to be about. Elicit from them any experiences that have had with cows. What do they already know about milk? Encourage them to volunteer any information they know. What products are made from milk? *(There are many possible examples.)* Ask the children to suggest anything they might like to find out about milk from the text.

2 Look at each picture. Discuss each picture one at a time. Ask the children to describe what each picture shows. *(A cow eating grass – the cow being milked – milk being collected – the tanker taking the milk – milk is pasteurised – milk is put into cartons.)* Then read the caption of each. How helpful is the discussion of each in contextualising the captions? Encourage the children to use phonological, contextual, grammatical and graphic knowledge to work out, predict and check the meanings of unfamiliar words and to make sense of what they read.

3 How is it possible to tell which picture comes next in the story? *(The pictures are numbered and have directional arrows.)*

4 After reading the text, ask the children to try and explain the process without access to the poster. Compare their versions with the original to check for any major variations.

Writing comprehension

1 Use reference books to research other similar 'stories', e.g. the story of a loaf of bread, an egg, a glass of water, etc. As a class, discuss the process of one and decide how to represent it in a few simple picture frames and captions, using the version on the poster as a model.

SENTENCE Level
Grammatical awareness

1 Ask the children to rewrite the captions by changing the subject of the sentences to the plural and noting what difference this makes to the verb. So 'A cow needs' becomes 'Cows need', and so on.

2 Provide the children with some simple sentences like 'a dog barks', 'a cat purrs', etc. Ask the children to change these into the plural, so 'dogs bark', 'cats purr'.

Sentence construction and punctuation

1 When working through the 'Writing comprehension' activity, draw attention to the way that the text for each picture is presented as a caption. Ensure that each simple sentence is written correctly with a capital letter at the beginning and a full stop at the end.

WORD Level
Spelling

1 Look at the word 'machine'. Point out to the class that the 'ch' has an unusual pronunciation. Can they think of other words? *(Other words you might like to suggest are 'chef', 'champagne', 'parachute', and 'brochure'.)* Also introduce the word 'Christmas' to show another way of pronouncing 'ch'. Can they think of other words? *(Other words you might like to suggest are 'school', 'echo', 'ache', 'stomach', 'character', 'chorus', 'architect', 'anchor' and 'scheme'.)*

2 Extend this activity to a consideration of words containing 'wh' and 'ph'. *(You might like to suggest 'which', 'where', 'what', 'who', 'when', 'why', 'wheel', 'white', 'wheat', 'whip' and 'whisk'; and 'alphabet', 'elephant', 'orphan', 'paragraph', 'geography', 'graph', 'nephew', 'phonic', 'phone' and 'phantom'.)*

Vocabulary extension

1 'Pasteurise' is an interesting word because the process gets its name from the discoverer of the process, Louis Pasteur. Can the children suggest other such words? Some which might be suggested are 'sandwich', 'Hoover', 'Braille' and 'cardigan'.

Related texts

'I Wonder How Bread is Made' by Neil Curtis

'Bread' by Diane Tippell

'The Magic Bus at the Waterworks' by Joanna Cole

'Water in the House' by Sue Palmer and Ron Murphy

'Chocolate' by Jacqueline Direen

'Chocolate' by Brian Moses (All about the commercial processing of chocolate.)

The Giant's Accidents

About the text

This poem consists of a story in patterned and predictable language. It involves a rather accident-prone giant. The last two lines read, "It can't get worse," he gave a grin, then slipped on a banana skin.'

Key Stage 1
Litercy Poster Pack 2

The Giant's Accidents

The giant stood up and hit his head;
he gasped and fell back on the bed.

The bed broke with a mighty crack –
he dropped right through and bumped his back.

He leapt up with a mighty roar
and knocked his elbow on the door.

He stiffened with the sudden pain,
and then he hit his head again.

He staggered around – the room was reeling
he slipped and crashed right through the ceiling.

To try to stop his sudden fall
he stretched his arm to grasp the wall.

The noise was heard all over town;
the whole house swayed and tumbled down.

He tunnelled up from underneath
with bits of floorboards in his teeth.

He shook his beard; some bricks dropped out
and gave his toes a nasty clout.

'It can't get worse,' he gave a grin,
then slipped on a banana skin.

From Another First Poetry Book by Charles Thomson

© Letts Educational 1998

Teaching opportunities at:

TEXT Level
Reading comprehension

1 Read the title of the poster. Discuss with the children what sort of accidents the giant might have. What sort of accidents have the children had? Encourage them to recount their accidents, relating where they were, what happened and how things turned out.

2 Explain that this is going to be a poem. What is the name of the poet? *(Charles Thomson.)* How is it possible to tell from the layout that it is a poem? Use words like verses, lines, rhyming, etc. *(It is in rhyming verse.)*

3 Read the poem to the class, acting it out and modulating your voice according to the story line. Ask the children to express their views on the poem after the first reading.

4 Discuss the setting – where did all the action take place? *(In the giant's house.)*

5 The poem consists of a series of mishaps. Ask the children to try and recall the sequence of events without reference to the poem. *(The giant hits his head – falls on the bed – drops through the bed onto the floor – knocks his elbow – hits his head – slips through the ceiling – knocks a wall down – bricks drop on his toes – slips on a banana skin.)*

6 Focus on words the children particularly like in the poem, perhaps 'staggered', 'mighty', 'gasped', 'crashed', etc. Encourage the children to study each word carefully and then to try and spell each without looking.

7 Find and compare other poems and stories about giants (see Related texts).

Writing comprehension

1 Extend the idea of the accident-prone giant. Think of different settings in which he continues having problems, e.g. in town, on the farm, at the seaside, etc. Brainstorm some ideas along the lines of the poem on the poster. Perhaps the poem could be done as a class poem, arising from the collective suggestions from the children.

SENTENCE Level
Grammatical awareness

1 Encourage the children to have fun practising and reading the poem aloud to each other, taking note of intonation and expression appropriate to the grammar and punctuation. Perhaps the readings could be accompanied by some form of role-play, too.

2 The poem has plenty of irregular past tenses in it. Read the poem to the class, deliberately making mistakes with these, and ask them to spot the mistakes and correct them. For example, 'the giant standed up and hitted his head'. (*The giant <u>stood</u> up and <u>hit</u> his head.*)

Sentence construction and punctuation

1 On the board, write a list of the sorts of things a giant might eat. For example, 'For his lunch, the giant had four pies, a sack of potatoes, twenty hamburgers, sixty chicken legs and three tubs of ice cream'. Point out how each item is separated with a comma, except for the item preceding the 'and'. Ask the children to make up their own lists and use commas correctly, e.g. 'things I have in my bag', 'things in my fridge', 'things I can see out of the window', etc.

WORD Level
Spelling

1 Look at the word 'floorboard' with the children. Note how it is made up of two shorter words joined together. It is called a compound word. Provide the children with a number of word , e.g. 'pan + cake = pancake' and ask them to make up some compound words and to use them in their own sentences. (*Some words you might use are 'milkman', 'teaspoon', 'handbag', 'suitcase', 'cloakroom', 'dustbin', 'tablecloth', 'sunshine', 'rainbow', 'snowman', 'footpath', 'farmyard' and 'toothbrush'.*)

Vocabulary extension

1 What images do the children have of giants? List some characteristics and words they associate with them on the board.

2 For a bit of fun, encourage them to provide the most gigantic (biggest) words they know. Make this into a class list of extremes.

Related texts

'Jack and the Beanstalk'
'Molly and the Giant' by Julia Jarman
'The BFG' by Roald Dahl

Mr Gumpy's Outing

About the text

This delightful well-known story by John Burningham is an excellent example of the use of patterned and predictable language being used effectively.

Teaching opportunities at:

TEXT Level
Reading comprehension

1 Read and discuss the title. What is an outing? *(It is a leisure trip.)* What outings have children been on? Where did they go? What did they do? Talk about the fact that outings are usually special in some way. What might Mr Gumpy's outing be? Where could he be going?

2 Read the story to the class, being careful to use different voices for each character.

3 What did each character ask Mr Gumpy? *(If they might go on his outing with him.)*

4 Read down to 'For a little while they all went along happily but then …' and stop. Cover up the rest of the text. Invite the children to suggest how the story might continue.

5 Read the first sentence of the paragraph again and then ' … the goat kicked …' Once more cover up the text and ask the children which animal will be mentioned next. Check with the text. Ask what the animal did and check with the text. Continue this pattern until all characters have been covered.

6 Finish reading the last paragraph and then ask the children to say what they thought of the story and why.

Key Stage 1
Literacy Poster Pack 2
Letts EDUCATIONAL

Mr Gumpy's Outing

One day Mr Gumpy went out in his boat.
'May we come with you?' said the children.
'Yes,' said Mr Gumpy, 'if you don't squabble.'
'Can I come along, Mr Gumpy?' said the rabbit.
'Yes, but don't hop about.'
'I'd like a ride,' said the cat.
'Very well,' said Mr Gumpy. 'But you're not to chase the rabbit.'
'Will you take me with you?' said the dog.
'Yes,' said Mr Gumpy. 'But don't tease the cat.'
'May I come please, Mr Gumpy?' said the pig.
'Very well, but don't muck about.'
'Have you a place for me?' said the sheep.
'Yes, but don't keep bleating.'
'Can we come too?' said the chickens.

'Yes, but don't flap,' said Mr Gumpy.
'Can you make room for me?' said the calf.
'Yes, if you don't trample about.'
'May I join you, Mr Gumpy?' said the goat.
'Very well, but don't kick.'
For a little while they all went along happily but then… the goat kicked… the calf trampled… the chickens flapped… the sheep bleated… the pig mucked about… the dog teased the cat… the cat chased the rabbit… the rabbit hopped… the children squabbled… the boat tipped… and into the water they fell.
Then Mr Gumpy and the goat and the calf and the chickens and the sheep and the pig and the dog and the cat and the rabbit and the children all swam to the bank and climbed out to dry in the hot sun.
'We'll walk home across the fields,' said Mr Gumpy. 'It's time for tea.'

From Mr Gumpy's Outing by John Burningham

© Letts Educational 1998   See Letts Literacy Activity Book 2 Term 2   page 12

Writing comprehension

1 Encourage the children to retell the story in their own words and then to check back against the actual text and compare versions. The story could perhaps be told in a series of picture frames using speech bubbles for dialogue. The frames could be joined with arrows like a flow diagram to reinforce the sequential aspects of the story.

2 Brainstorm some words that describe Mr Gumpy, and then get children to write a short description of the sort of man he was.

SENTENCE Level
Grammatical awareness

1 Give the children the following pattern and ask them to follow it for each character: Mr Gumpy told the children not to squabble but the children squabbled. Draw attention to the way the verb ending changes. Notice the way this affects the spelling of some of the root words and point this out to the class.

Sentence construction and punctuation

1 Ask the children to identify all the speech marks in the text and say who is speaking each time. *(The children, Mr Gumpy, the rabbit, Mr Gumpy, the cat, Mr Gumpy, the dog, Mr Gumpy, the pig, Mr Gumpy, the sheep, Mr Gumpy, the chickens, Mr Gumpy, the calf, Mr Gumpy, the goat, Mr Gumpy and Mr Gumpy.)* Ask them to repeat exactly the words each character said.

2 Ask the children to find all the question marks in the text. *(There are eight examples.)* Encourage them to explain when they need to use question marks.

WORD Level
Spelling

1 Mr Gumpy was unhappy when the animals started misbehaving. Write the word 'unhappy' on the board. Draw attention to the effect adding the prefix 'un-' to the word has. *(It makes it the opposite.)* Write the word 'disagree' on the board. Follow the same process with this. *(Again it reverses the meaning.)* Write the words 'well', 'fair', 'pack', 'cover', 'load', 'agree', 'trust', 'place', 'arm' and 'honest' on the board. Ask the children to decide whether the prefix 'un-' or 'dis-' should be placed in front of each. *('Unwell', 'unfair', 'unpack', 'uncover', 'unload', 'disagree', 'distrust', 'displace', 'disarm' and 'dishonest'.)* Ask the children to use the words in sentences to show they know their meanings.

Vocabulary extension

1 The spelling activity involves using prefixes to create opposites of words. Follow this up by asking children for the opposites of some of the words in the text such as 'come', 'swim', 'take', 'walk', 'dry' and 'hot'. *(From this list, those that have opposites are: 'go', 'bring', 'wet' and 'cold'.)* Add some more words to the list from other sources. Ask the children to complete simple sentences such as 'The sun is hot but ...', then suggest they think of something that is opposite and complete the sentence '... but ice is cold'.

Related texts

Other titles by John Burningham:

'The Car Ride'

'Mr Gumpy's Motor Car'

'Aldo'

'Animal Chatter'

'Avocado Baby'

Borka: The Adventures of a Goose with No Feathers'

'Come Away from the Water, Shirley'

Two Poems to Enjoy

About the text

The two poems on this poster are both by significant children's poets. 'When I Was One' is by A. A. Milne and 'What is Pink?' is by Christina Rossetti.

Teaching opportunities at:

TEXT Level
Reading comprehension

1 Read and discuss each poem, one at a time. Read 'When I Was One' first and ask the children for their immediate responses to the poem. Did they like it or not? Ask them to try and explain their responses.

2 Discuss the poet. Have the children ever read anything else by him (see Unit 3.6 'Winnie-the-Pooh')? Discuss the way the poem is set out and some of its features. *(It is in verses of two lines each and the pairs of lines are rhyming couplets.)*

3 Talk about some of the verses. Ask the children to suggest what 'When I was one, I had just begun,' means. Encourage them to explain what message the poet was trying to get across. *(Answers will depend on the children's interpretation.)*

4 Ask the children to recount some of their earliest memories about growing up, or perhaps their memories of a younger relation. What sort of things are babies and toddlers able to do? How does this change as you grow up?

5 Read 'What is Pink?' to the class. Follow the same process as for 'When I Was One' by asking them to express their views about the poem; to discuss the features of the poem; to consider the overall theme of the poem; and to link it to children's personal experiences by asking them what they associate with each colour.

6 If possible, find and read other poems by these two famous poets for enjoyment and comparison (see Related texts).

Writing comprehension

1 Both poems lend themselves well to extension, such as 'When I was seven' and 'What is brown?', or to children writing their own versions of the poems along the same lines.

2 Encourage the children to make copies of their favourite poems in their best handwriting and to illustrate them, possibly making a class anthology of favourite poems.

Key Stage 1
Literacy Poster Pack 2
Letts EDUCATIONAL

Two Poems to Enjoy

When I Was One

When I was One,
I had just begun.
When I was Two,
I was nearly new.
When I was Three,
I was hardly Me.
When I was Four,
I was not much more.
When I was Five,
I was just alive.
But now I'm Six, I'm as clever as clever.
So I think I'll be six now for ever and ever.
From The Now We Are Six Collection by A. A. Milne

What is Pink?

What is pink? A rose is pink
By the fountain's brink.
What is red? A poppy's red
In its barley bed.
What is blue? The sky is blue
Where the clouds float through.
What is white? A swan is white
Sailing in the light.
What is yellow? Pears are yellow,
Rich, and ripe, and mellow.
What is green? The grass is green,
With small flowers between.
What is violet? Clouds are violet
In the summer twilight.
What is orange?
Why, an orange is orange,
Just an orange!
By Christina Rossetti

© Letts Educational 1998   See Letts Literacy Activity Book 2 Term 2 page 14

SENTENCE Level
Grammatical awareness

1 Encourage the children to practise and read aloud the poems to each other, taking into account their grammar and punctuation. Suggest the other children comment on how well the poems were read in terms of conveying their meanings and using appropriate expression.

2 Try rewriting parts of the poems but changing the noun or pronoun into the plural, and noting how this affects the verbs. For example, 'When <u>we were</u> one, we had just begun', 'What is pink? Roses <u>are pink</u>', and so on.

Sentence construction and punctuation

1 Draw attention to the use of commas in the two poems. Ask the children what signal they give to the reader when reading aloud. *(They act as a pause and indicate a continuation of the sentence.)* Read the poems aloud to the class ignoring the commas, and then taking them into account. Can the children hear the difference?

WORD Level
Spelling

1 Discuss the fact that we can break longer words down into smaller parts called syllables. Use some two-syllable words from the first poem to demonstrate, like 'begun', 'nearly', 'hardly', 'alive' and 'clever'. Say the words slowly and tap out the beat of each syllable as you do so. Each of the given words consists of two syllables. *('Be/gun', 'near/ly', 'hard/ly', 'a/live' and 'cle/ver'.)* Try the clapping syllable beats test to check. Sometimes saying the words like a robot or Dalek helps bring home the point! Ask the children to find as many two-syllable words as possible in the second poem. *('Foun/tain', 'pop/py', 'bar/ley', 'sail/ing', 'yel/low', 'mel/low', 'flow/ers', 'bet/ween', 'sum/mer', 'twi/light' and 'o/range'.)*

Vocabulary extension

1 Draw the children's attention to the colour words. Sort these into broad colours and shades, e.g. 'burnt sienna' would come under brown. Collect some manufacturer's paint charts and discuss the names they give to colours.

Related texts

Some titles by A. A. Milne:

'The Christopher Robin Verse Book'

'The Hums of Pooh'

'Stories of Winnie-the-Pooh Together with Favourite Poems'

For a poem about colour:

'Poems About Colour' selected by Amanda Earl and Danielle Sensier

An Animal Dictionary

About the text

This poster features a page from an animal dictionary, consisting of several animals, arranged in alphabetical order, their pictures and a simple definition for each.

Key Stage 1
Literacy Poster Pack 2
Letts EDUCATIONAL

An Animal Dictionary

	alligator	An alligator is a large reptile that lives in rivers and swamps in America and China.
	bear	A bear is a very big, heavy, wild animal with thick fur.
	camel	A camel comes from countries with hot deserts. They can go for a long time without eating.
	deer	A deer is an animal that eats grass. Some deers have antlers. Deers can run fast.
	elephant	The elephant is the largest land animal. It has a trunk and two tusks. It lives in Africa and India.
	fox	A fox looks like a dog with a long bushy tail. It lives in the wild.
	giraffe	A giraffe is a tall animal with a very long neck and long legs. It comes from Africa.
	hedgehog	A hedgehog is a small animal with prickles on its back.

© Letts Educational 1998   See *Letts Literacy Activity Book 2 Term 2* page 16

Teaching opportunities at:

TEXT Level
Reading comprehension

1 Ask the children to try and explain in their own words what a dictionary is. Encourage them to offer explanations, including the fact that it consists of a list of words which are arranged in alphabetical order; it usually tells you what each word means; it helps with spelling.

2 Look at each entry, one at a time. Cover up the name and definition. Look at the picture and ask the children to name each animal. Reveal the name and check if they were right. Use each animal's name as an opportunity to apply phonological and spelling skills. Ask the children to say what they know about each animal. Reveal and read the definition for each, introducing and using the word 'definition' as you do so. Use phonological, grammatical, contextual and graphic knowledge to work out, predict and check the meanings of unfamiliar words and to make sense of what is read. As each new animal is revealed, stress the alphabetical nature of the organisation of their names. Before moving on from one animal to the next, ask the children if they can think of any other animals beginning with that same letter that could have been included.

3 Review the children's knowledge of the alphabet by saying the letters in order and holding alphabet quizzes.

4 Encourage the children to refer to and use class dictionaries and to become familiar with their layout and organisation.

5 Look at and discuss a range of other texts that are organised alphabetically. You might suggest indexes, glossaries, encyclopedias, telephone directories, the class register, and so on.

Writing comprehension

1 Ask the children to write and explain the usefulness of a dictionary.

2 Make class dictionaries and glossaries of special interest words, giving explanations and definitions, perhaps linked to class topics or derived from stories and poems.

SENTENCE Level
Grammatical awareness

1 Encourage the children to read their own writing for grammatical sense (coherence) and accuracy (agreement); to identify errors and to suggest alternative constructions.

Sentence construction and punctuation

1 Through the focus on dictionaries, encourage the children to investigate and recognise different ways of presenting texts. They might use bold or underlining, headings and sub-headings, clear page structure for accessibility, and such like.

2 Select some of the definitions on the poster and jumble up the words order. Ask the children to work out and write the words in the correct order so they make sense.

WORD Level
Spelling

1 'Alligator' and 'badger' end in 'or' and 'er'. Challenge the children to find the names of some other animals ending in a similar way. *(There are many possible examples.)*

2 Write the names of the animals from the poster on the board. Make a few deliberate mistakes. Ask the children to check the spellings against the actual spellings and correct any that are wrong.

3 Study the name of each animal one at a time. Ask the children to identify any tricky bits in each word. How can they remember them? *(Suggest underlining unusual parts of the word; looking for small words within larger words; looking for common spelling patterns; thinking of other similar words; breaking the word down into parts and thinking about the meaning. Remind the children of the 'Look, say, cover, write, check' strategy.)*

Vocabulary extension

1 Give the children sets of other animal names (four or five at most in each set) and ask them to place them in alphabetical order according to the first letter.

2 Ask the children to write a definition for some animals not included in the dictionary page on the poster. Make sure the children check their definitions in a dictionary.

Related texts

'An Imaginary Menagerie' by Roger McGough (An A–Z of extraordinary animals)

'Dictionary of Nature' by Davie Burnie

'The Children's Visual Dictionary' by Jane Bunting

'Young Reader's Dictionary' by David Smith and Susan Cassin

Why Do Dogs Chase Cars?

About the text

This is a modern story from Northern Ghana which suggests that the reason dogs chase cars is because, a long time ago, a taxi driver cheated a dog out of its change – and dogs now spend their whole time chasing cars, looking for that taxi driver!

Teaching opportunities at:

TEXT Level
Reading comprehension

1 Look at the title and the illustrations. Ask the children to guess where the story is set and to try and answer the question in the title. *(Northern Ghana, and dogs chase cars to find the taxi driver who cheated them.)* Tell them they can check their guesses as they read the story.

2 Look next at the acknowledgement at the bottom of the text. *(This answers where the story is set.)* What sort of story is it going to be? *(It is a traditional story.)*

3 Read the story with the class down to the part where the dog is about to get out of the taxi. Ask the children if they think anything different is going to happen. Read on and check their guesses!

4 Read the rest of the story. At the end, ask the children what they think of the taxi driver.

5 Ask the children what they thought of the story. Did it make them smile? Why?

6 Encourage the children to retell the story in their own words without reference to the text. Check their versions against the text for accuracy. (The story also lends itself quite well to role-playing and being acted out.)

Writing comprehension

1 This type of story lends itself well as a model for stimulating and structuring other stories in a similar vein, e.g. 'Why do humming birds hum?', 'Why do hyenas laugh?', etc. Encourage the children to use three characters and one 'baddy', and to incorporate some of the language used, like 'Some time ago', 'So now you know', etc.

SENTENCE Level
Grammatical awareness

1 Read the story again to the children but make deliberate mistakes with the past tenses of the irregular verbs in it. For example, 'Some time ago, when cars first comed to the roads'. Ask the children to put up their hands when they hear a mistake and to supply the correct verb in its place.

Sentence construction and punctuation

1 Supply lists of four or so animals for the children. Ask them to write each list and use commas correctly to punctuate them, as with 'A dog, a donkey, a goat and a hyena'.

WORD Level
Spelling

1 Write the words 'where', 'their', and 'fare' on the board. Ask the children to find each word in the text. Discuss what they have in common. *(They all contain the same sound.)* Ask the children to suggest as many other words as possible which rhyme. Categorise them according to their common letter patterns.

Vocabulary extension

1 Ask the children to explain the difference between the following pairs of words: 'hair/hare', 'mare/mayor', 'bare/bear', 'fare/fair', 'pear/pair', 'stare/stair', 'there/their' and 'where/wear'. *(They have the same sound but different letter patterns.)*

2 Select some of the words from the text and ask the children to supply an antonym (opposite) for each. You might try 'comes', 'last', 'out', 'took', etc. *('Go', 'first', 'in' and 'brought'.)*

Related texts

'Anansi and the Magic Yams: A Folk Tale from Ghana' by Joanne Troughton

'Anno's Aesop: A Book of Fables by Aesop and Mr. Fox' by Mitsumasa Anno

'Aesop's Fables' by Anne Gatti

The 'Just So Stories' by Rudyard Kipling

The Caterpillar

About the text

This is a particularly interesting poster because it combines two distinctively different types of writing – a rhyme explaining the metamorphosis of a caterpillar into a butterfly and a flow diagram to explain the process in factual language as a contrast.

Teaching opportunities at:

TEXT Level
Reading comprehension

1 Before looking at the poster, ask if any of the children have read 'The Hungry Caterpillar' by Eric Carle. Ask them to explain what happens in it. Follow this by a discussion of what the children know about the lifecycle of a butterfly.

2 Look at the series of pictures and captions on the poster surrounding the rhyme. Explain that they tell the story in pictures and words. Ask the children where to begin. *(At number 1, with laying eggs.)*

3 Read each picture and caption one at a time. Discuss any difficult or unfamiliar words, asking the children to use a variety of cues to unlock their meaning. Discuss how much each picture helps the reader understand the accompanying caption. Draw attention to the heading of each picture which summarises the stage in one or two words.

4 Encourage the children to study the flow diagram for a short period, then cover the poster. Ask them to try and recall the six stages.

5 Next, read the rhyme with the class. (This is very easy to accompany with appropriate

Key Stage 1
Literacy Poster Pack 2
Letts EDUCATIONAL

The Caterpillar

1 *Laying eggs*

2 *Hatching*

3 *Eating*

A caterpillar crawled to the top of a tree.
"I think I'll take a nap," said he.
So – under a leaf he began to creep
To spin a cocoon;
Then he fell asleep.
All winter he slept in his cocoon bed,
Till Spring came along one day and said,
"Wake up, wake up, little sleepyhead.
Wake up, it's time to get out of bed."
So – he opened his eyes that sunshiny day.
Lo! He was a butterfly – and flew away!

From Hand Rhymes by Marc Brown

6 *Emerging*

4 *Making a cocoon*

5 *Sleeping*

© Letts Educational 1996   See *Letts Literacy Activity Book 2 Term 2 page 20*

hand gestures, which children can join in.) Read it again, and ask the children to match the different parts of the rhyme to the flow diagram pictures.

6 Find and read other rhymes and poems about insects and elicit children's opinions of them (see 'Related texts').

Writing comprehension

1 Encourage the children do some research into the life cycle of frogs. Translate this into a flow diagram with the class, through discussion, and using the diagram on the poster as a model.

2 Make up a poem about the life cycle of the frog in the same style as the rhyme about the caterpillar.

SENTENCE Level
Grammatical awareness

1 Use the theme of the way insects move to focus on subject/verb agreements. For example, 'a caterpillar crawls but caterpillars crawl', 'a beetle scuttles but beetles scuttle', etc.

Sentence construction and punctuation

1 Link this with the Writing comprehension, point 1. Encourage children to write their captions in correct sentences, beginning with capital letters and ending with full stops. Ensure they proof-read their work when complete to check for this.

WORD Level
Spelling

1 Find the words 'butterfly' and 'sunshine' in the text. Do word sums with each to show how they are made, for example 'butter + cup = buttercup'. Introduce these as compound words. Give the children the first word of several compound words and ask them to supply the missing last part of the word. You might like to try 'rain' ('bow', 'drop', 'water'), 'foot' ('ball', 'path', 'step'), and so on.

Vocabulary extension

1 The rhyme mentions spring and winter. Ask the children to supply (and spell correctly) the seasons in order from spring. Brainstorm words, phrases and sentences about the characteristics of each season.

2 Now ask the children to supply (and spell correctly) the months of the year and the days of the week.

Related texts

'Is a Caterpillar Ticklish?' ed. by
Adrian Rumble

'Mini Beasties' ed. Michael Rosen (This is a wonderful collection of poems about creepy crawlies.)

A non-fiction title:
'Minibeasts' by Gerald Legg

Ma Liang and the Magic Brush

About the text

This traditional Chinese story tells the tale of Ma Liang, a poor Chinese boy. Ma Liang loves drawing but is too poor to buy a brush. One day, an old man appears and gives him a brush and it turns out to be magic.

Teaching opportunities at:

TEXT Level
Reading comprehension

1 Read the title and look at the illustrations together. Ask the children to suggest what they think the story might be about. Is it possible to tell anything about the setting from the illustrations? *(The illustrations of the characters and props clearly suggest a Far-east Asian setting.)*

2 Read the story to the class to check their predictions. Were they right?

3 Ask the children to identify the three main characters in the story and to comment on each one. Make sure they use information in the text, the illustrations and their imaginations. What does each character look like? What qualities do they have? Are they kind, or are they cruel? What sort of things do they do? *(Answers will depend on the children's interpretation.)*

4 Ask the children to suggest other ways in which the story might have ended.

5 Prompt the children to express their own opinions about the story. Were they glad the king got his comeuppance? Why?

Key Stage 1
Literacy Poster Pack 2

Letts
EDUCATIONAL

Ma Liang and the Magic Brush

Once upon a time there was a boy who liked drawing but he was too poor to buy a brush. One night he said to himself, 'If only I had a brush, I could draw pictures for the poor people in my village.'

Suddenly an old man with a long white beard appeared. 'Don't be frightened,' he said. 'Here's a brush for you. But you must only draw pictures for poor people with it.'

Ma Liang began to draw a hen, and as he did so it changed into a real hen. 'Wow!' he said. 'This brush must be magic!'

Then he saw a poor woman cutting wood. 'You need an axe,' he said. So he drew an axe and it changed into a real one.

Next he saw a poor farmer pulling a plough. 'You need a buffalo to pull your plough,' Ma Liang said. So he drew a buffalo and it changed into a real buffalo.

'Thank you. You are very kind,' the farmer said to Ma Liang.

Soon the king heard about Ma Liang's magic brush. 'Draw me a tree with gold coins hanging on it,' he ordered.

'You have plenty of gold. You don't need any more,' Ma Liang replied. The king was angry. 'Throw him in prison!' he cried. His soldiers caught hold of Ma Liang, threw him in prison and locked the door.

'If I had a key I could unlock the door,' Ma Liang said. So he drew a key and it changed into a real key. He opened the door quietly and escaped. When the king discovered that Ma Liang had got away, he got on his horse and chased him with his soldiers.

Ma Liang said, 'I need a horse.' So he drew one and it changed into a real horse. He jumped on it and galloped away.

A traditional story from China

© Letts Educational 1998   See *Letts Literacy Activity Book 2 Term 2* page 22

Writing comprehension

1 Encourage the children to tell the story in their own words. This might be done as a series of picture frames with captions, like a comic.

2 Ask the children to choose one of the characters from the story and to write a character profile of him or her. Use the same questions as Reading comprehension, point 3 above to help children structure the profile.

3 Ask the children to suggest other ways in which the story might have ended.

SENTENCE Level
Grammatical awareness

1 Provide the children with a few 'doctored' sentences from the story in which the verbs have been changed so that subject and verb disagree. For example, 'Once upon a time there were a boy'. Make sure the children rewrite the sentences correctly. (*Once upon a time there was a boy.*)

Sentence construction and punctuation

1 Provide the children with some sentence beginnings, based on the story. The children have to think of a suitable ending for each sentence, ensuring they use correct punctuation.

WORD Level
Spelling

1 Ask the children to go through the text and write down all the verbs they can spot which end in '-ing' or '-ed'. Write these on the board. (*'-ing': 'drawing', 'cutting', 'pulling', 'hanging', 'getting'; '-ed': 'liked', 'appeared', 'frightened', 'changed', 'ordered', 'replied', 'cried', 'locked', 'opened', 'escaped', 'discovered', 'chased', 'jumped', 'galloped', 'stopped', 'disappeared'.*) Study each word, one at a time and ask the children what the shorter word is that it has grown from. (*'Draw', 'cut', 'pull', 'hang', 'get', 'like', 'appear', 'frighten', 'change', 'order', 'reply', 'cry', 'lock', 'open', 'escape', 'discover', 'chase', 'jump', 'gallop', 'stop', 'disappear'.*) Which of the 'root' words has remained the same and simply added the suffix? (*'Draw', 'pull', 'hang', 'appear', 'frighten', 'order', 'lock', 'open', 'discover', 'jump', 'gallop', 'disappear'.*) Which words have changed in some way when the suffix was added? (*'Cut', 'get', 'like', 'change', 'reply', 'cry', 'escape', 'chase', 'stop'.*)

Vocabulary extension

1 Select some of the words from the story and ask the children to think of some synonyms (words with the same meaning), such as 'liked' – 'enjoyed', 'loved'.

2 Select some of the words from the story and ask the children to think of some antonyms (words with the opposite meaning).

Related texts

'The Moon Lady' by Amy Tan and Gretchen Shields

'Aladdin' retold by Andrew Lang

'Monkey and the Water' by Joanna Troughton

'Wishbones: A Folk Tale from China' by Barbara Kerr Wilson

Stories from around the world:

'Tales from Around the World: Stories to Read Aloud' by Saviour Pirotta

Rhymes Around the World

About the text

The poster consists of four very different rhymes from around the world, offering plenty of scope for discussion and enjoyment.

Teaching opportunities at:

TEXT Level
Reading comprehension

1 Read the title and look at where each rhyme comes from before reading them. If appropriate, find the places in an atlas.

2 Read 'Susie, Susie' and ask the children to say what they thought of it. What sort of a rhyme was it? Was it funny or serious? *(Explain that it is a nonsense rhyme and is intended to make the reader smile.)* Which words rhymed in it? *('Toe/Mexico', 'hair/underwear'.)* Encourage the children to read it aloud several times, paying attention to the punctuation.

3 Read 'Hickety, bickety, pease, scone'. Encourage the children to use all available cues to guess what the word 'gang' means. *(The last line might be questioning whether the man will join the navy – as a crow's nest is the look out box, high up the main mast on old sailing ships.)* Notice how the first line is really just doggerel without any real meaning – a common feature of rhymes (note the first line of 'Ting-a-ling-bone', too.) Why was this rhyme more difficult to understand? (Discuss the use of some words commonly only used by Scottish people.)

4 Read 'Ting-a-ling-bone'. Which animals feature in this rhyme? *(Goats, hens and dogs.)* Which words rhyme? *('Bone/home', 'hen/then', 'well/bell'.)* Notice how the rhyme tells a kind of story or sequence of events.

Key Stage 1
Literacy Poster Pack 2
Letts EDUCATIONAL

Rhymes Around the World

Susie Susie
Susie Susie suck your toe,
All the way to Mexico.
When you get there, cut your hair,
And don't forget your underwear.
A traditional poem from the USA

Hickety, bickety, pease, scone
Hickety, bickety, pease, scone,
Where shall this poor Scotsman gang?
Will he gang east, or will he gang west,
Or will he gang to the crow's nest?
A traditional poem from Scotland

Ting-a-ling-bone
Ting-a-ling-bone! Ting-a-ling-bone!
A fire broke out in the little goat's home.
A bucketful of water was fetched by the hen,
To put the fire out if she could, and then

The dogs from the farmhouse came as well,
They were bringing a ladder and ringing a bell.

Ting-a-ling-bone! Ting-a-ling-bone!
We'll put out the fire in the little goat's home.
A traditional poem from the Caribbean

Titli
Ek phool par bahti titli
Hans ka baccho se ye boli
'Pankh dekh lo, nit aungi
Tang kiya to urd jaungi.'

Butterfly sitting on a flower
Smiles to the children and says,
'I'll come every day. See my wings,
If you irritate me, I'll fly away.'
A traditional Hindi rhyme from India

© Letts Educational 1998   See *Letts Literacy Activity Book 2* Term 2   page 24

Ask the children to read this rhyme aloud – it is good for acting out, too!

5 Read 'Titli'. Ask the children what language they think the left hand version is in. *(It is in Hindi.)* Explain that the right hand version is a translation into English. Ask the children to articulate their responses to the rhyme. Does the English version actually rhyme? *(No.)* Does the Hindi version? *(Yes.)* Discuss why this might be. Ask the children to suggest what 'Titli' might mean.

Writing comprehension

1 Have fun adding some more lines to 'Susie Susie', or make up another, similar, nonsense rhyme.

2 Read aloud a selection of nursery and other rhymes and ask the children to write out and illustrate their favourites for a class anthology.

SENTENCE Level

Grammatical awareness

1 Make up some nonsense sentences in which the order of the words is jumbled up. Ask the children to sort the words into the correct order and write each sentence again so it makes sense.

Sentence construction and punctuation

1 Hold a 'punctuation spotting' competition. How many full stops, commas, question marks and exclamation marks can the children find in the rhymes on the poster? *(Seven full stops, two question marks and four exclamation marks.)*

WORD Level
Spelling

1 Use the words 'butterfly', 'underwear', 'farm-house' from the rhymes to study compound words. Notice how each word is in fact made up of two shorter words. *('Butter + fly', 'under + wear', 'farm + house'.)* Ask the children to look through their reading books and note any other compound words. Draw up a collective class list.

2 Look at the word 'bucketful' in 'Ting-a-ling-bone'. Explain that it really means 'a bucket full'. Point out that we can write it as one word, but when 'full' comes at the end of a word it loses one 'l'. Ask the children to suggest other words with the '-ful' suffix. *(For example, 'useful', 'careful', 'helpful', 'painful', 'hopeful', 'powerful', 'restful', 'thoughtful' and 'colourful'.)*

Vocabulary extension

1 Use the '-ful' words from Spelling point 2. Show the children how they can be made into antonyms (words with the opposite meaning) by substituting '-less' for '-ful', as with 'helpful' and 'helpless'.

Related texts

'Tickle Your Tummy' chosen by Judith Elkin and Carlton Duncan

'No Hickory, No Dickory, No Dock' by John Agard and Grace Nichols (Caribbean poetry)

'The Kiskadee Queen' ed. Faustin Charles and Liz Toft (A collection of Caribbean, Indian, African-American and African nursery rhymes.)

'Not a Copper Penny in Me House' by Monica Gunning (Poems from the Caribbean)

'Poetry Jump-in: An Anthology of Black Poetry' ed. Grace Nichols

Suggested Scottish fairy stories:

'Scottish Fairy Tales' by Grant Campbell

Everybody Said No!

About the text

This extract is taken from a story by Sheila Lavelle. It is rather like a modern-day version of the traditional story 'The Little Red Hen'. It has an in-built predictability about it – whenever Mrs Mudd asks for help, everybody says no!

Teaching opportunities at:

TEXT Level
Reading comprehension

1 Look at the title. Ask the children if any of them have read 'Little Red Hen'. If they have, ask them to recount it simply in their own words. If they haven't, if appropriate, briefly give a summary of the story. (In this story, Little Red Hen plants some seeds, nurtures them, watches them grow, harvests the wheat, mills it into flour, makes it into bread and bakes it. At every stage of the story, she asks her friends for help but they say no – except when she asks if they would like to help eat the loaf!) Tell the children that this extract is from a story with a similar theme.

2 Draw attention to the acknowledgement to the author at the bottom of the poster. Discuss what an author does. Ask the children if they have any favourite authors.

3 Read the first section of the story to the class. Stop and ask the children to point out which characters are which in the accompanying illustration. If necessary, reread the section again to go over what individual characters are doing. Discuss how old the Mudd children might be. Who is Hoover? *(Hoover is the cat.)*

Key Stage 1
Literacy Poster Pack 2
Letts EDUCATIONAL

Everybody Said No!

One day, Mrs Mudd bought an apple tree in the market and brought it home.
"Look at this lovely apple tree!" she said to her big family.
"Would anybody like to help me plant it in the garden?"
But everybody said no! Mr Mudd was very busy reading his newspaper. John and Sally had to do their homework. Dick was brushing his teeth. Betty was washing her doll. Hoover was watching the goldfish swimming around in the bowl. And Little Joe was just too little.
So Mrs Mudd had to plant the apple tree all by herself.
In the summer the sun was very hot and the earth dry and hard. The leaves on the little apple tree began to droop and wilt.
"Look at our poor little apple tree," said Mrs Mudd to her big family. "Would anybody like to help me water it?"
But everybody said no! Mr Mudd was busy snoozing in the deck chair in the garden. John and Sally were painting a picture. Dick had to polish his shoes. Betty was knitting new pink socks for her doll. Hoover was climbing the lilac tree. And Little Joe was just too little.
So Mrs Mudd had to water the little apple tree all by herself.
In the autumn the apple tree was covered in big juicy apples.
"Look at all the apples on our tree!" said Mrs Mudd. "Would anybody like to help me pick them?"
But everybody said no!...

*From Everybody Said No!
by Sheila Lavelle*

© Letts Educational 1998   See *Letts Literacy Activity Book 2* Term 3   page 6

4 Read the middle section down to the part where Mrs Mudd asks for help. Cover the text and the illustration and ask the children what they think the answer will be. What might each character be doing? Reveal the text and the picture and check children's predictions.

5 Read the last section of the story. Ask the children to suggest what everyone might be doing this time (the extract is deliberately stopped at this point to encourage prediction).

6 What do the children think of the family's response to Mrs Mudd each time? Is it fair? Is it kind? This could lead into a general discussion of running a home and whose responsibility is what. Should everyone play a part? How?

Writing comprehension

1 Ask the children to suggest how the story might continue. What is going to happen to the apples? Do the children think everyone continues to say no, even when the apple pie is baked?

SENTENCE Level
Grammatical awareness

1 Suggest the children rewrite a section of the story, but write the verbs incorrectly, e.g. 'One day, Mrs Mudd buyed an apple tree in the market and bringed it home'. Ask the children to read and correct the verbs. *(One day, Mrs Mudd <u>bought</u> an apple tree and <u>brought</u> it home.)*

Sentence construction and punctuation

1 Draw three simple pictures of Mrs Mudd on the board, with a large speech bubble coming from each picture. Ask the children to find and write the exact words Mrs Mudd said in each section of the story. Use this activity to draw attention to the way speech marks are used to enclose the actual words people say.

2 Ask the children to find examples of questions being asked in the text. *(There are many examples they might choose.)* Note the way question marks are used to signal this. Take one section of the story and ask the children to turn the statements about the Mudd family members into questions. So 'Mr Mudd was reading the newspaper' could become 'What was Mr Mudd reading?'

3 Find all the names of the characters in the story. Explain that when a person's name is written, it should always begin with a capital letter. Ask the children to list five boys' and five girls' names in the class, ensuring capital letters are used correctly.

WORD Level
Spelling

1 Use the words 'homework', 'newspaper' and 'goldfish' from the text to revise work on compound words. Write these as word sums, e.g. 'gold + fish = goldfish'. Ask the children to suggest other compound words or to find more in reading books. Encourage them to write them as word sums as an aid to spelling.

Vocabulary extension

1 Choose some words from the text and ask the children to provide some synonyms (words with similar meanings), e.g. 'snoozing' – 'dozing', 'sleeping', 'having a nap', and so on.

Related texts

'The Little Red Hen'

Other titles by Sheila Lavelle:

'The Apple Pie Alien'

'The Big Stink'

'The Boggy Day Marathon'

'Calamity with the Fiend'

'Copycat'

'Fetch the Slipper'

'Ursula by the Sea'

The Brute Family

About the text

In the middle of a dark and shadowy woods lived a little family of Brutes. They were brutes by name and by nature. This extract from Russell Hoban's charming story tells of the discovery of a little lost good feeling (which, in the full story, leads to the transformation of the family).

Teaching opportunities at:

TEXT Level
Reading comprehension

1 Look at the title and the illustration. Ask if anyone can explain what a brute is. *(A brute is any animal, except humans, and it is a word with coarse connotations.)* Discuss what is happening in the picture and ask the children to describe the members of the Brute family. What do they think they are going to be like in the story?

2 Read the story to the class to the end of the third paragraph. Ask the children to say what they think of the family. Discuss each member. What sort of person is he or she? What words do the children think best describe the characters?

3 Discuss the setting. Where do the family live? *(They live in a dark and shadowy wood.)* What is their home like? *(Use the illustration and the text for information and encourage the children to think imaginatively.)*

4 Read the last paragraph. What effect did Baby Brute's discovery have on him? *(He suddenly and unexpectedly felt happy.)*

5 Ask the children what they thought of the story. If possible, find and read other extracts or books by Russell Hoban for comparison. (See Related texts.)

Key Stage 1
Literacy Poster Pack 2
Letts EDUCATIONAL

The Brute Family

In the middle of a dark and shadowy wood lived a little family of Brutes. There were Papa Brute, Mama Brute, Brother and Sister Brute and Baby Brute. Baby Brute howled between spoonfuls. Brother and Sister Brute kicked each other under the table, and Mama and Papa made faces while they ate.

After breakfast Papa Brute took up his sack and went off to gather sticks and stones. Mama stayed at home to thump the furniture and bang the pots and scold the baby. And Brother and Sister Brute pushed and shoved and punched and pinched their way to school.

In the evenings Mama served a stew of sticks and stones, and the family ate it with growls and grumblings. Then they groaned and went to sleep. That was how they lived. They never laughed and said, "Delightful!" They never smiled and said, "How lovely!"

… Then one day Baby Brute found a little lost wandering good feeling in a field of daisies, and he caught it up and put it in his tiny pocket. And he felt so good that he laughed and said, "How lovely."

From The Little Brute Family by Russell Hoban

© Letts Educational 1998   See *Letts Literacy Activity Book 2 Term 3 page 8*

Writing comprehension

1 In the story, baby Brute takes the 'good feeling' home with him – with amazing consequences. As a class, discuss some of the things that might happen next. Write some ideas on the board. Ask the children to continue the story in their own words.

2 Read some of the Roger Hargreaves' 'Mr Men' stories and ask the children to write their own versions.

SENTENCE Level
Grammatical awareness

1 Make up some sentences about the Brute family, but include some deliberate mistakes with the gender of some of the pronouns. For example, 'Sister Brute was not kind to his brother'. Ask the children to identify and correct the mistakes. *(Sister Brute was not kind to* <u>her</u> *brother.)*

Sentence construction and punctuation

1 Write some simple sentences about the story. Do not use capitals or full stops. Ask the children to punctuate each sentence appropriately.

WORD Level
Spelling

1 Use the words 'spoonful' and 'delightful' from the text. Explain that whenever the word 'full' is added to a word ('spoonful' literally means 'a spoon full') only one 'l' is required. Give the children the following words and ask them to add the suffix '-ful' to each: 'play', 'help', 'wonder', 'cheer', 'joy', 'truth', 'use' and 'care'. *('Playful', 'helpful', 'wonderful', 'cheerful', 'joyful', 'truthful', 'useful' and 'careful'.)* Then ask them to make up sentences containing each word.

2 Look at the word 'lovely' in the text. Give children the following words and ask them to add the suffix '-ly' to each: 'clever', 'slow', 'quick', 'quiet', 'fair', 'willing' and 'careful'. *('Cleverly', 'slowly', 'quickly', 'quietly', 'fairly', 'willingly' and 'carefully'.)* Now ask the children to make up sentences using each word.

Vocabulary extension

1 Choose some words from the text, such as 'dark', 'howl', 'thump', 'push', 'ate', 'grumble', 'groan' and 'tiny'. Ask the children to suggest some synonyms (words with a similar meaning) for each one.

Related texts
Other Russell Hoban titles:
'The Mouse and His Child'
'The Ace Dragon'
'A Baby Sister for Frances'
'Bedtime for Frances'
'Dinner at Alberta's'

The Guest

About the text

Owl is sitting nice and snug in front of his fire when Winter comes knocking at the door and rushing in, creating havoc. It is a very unwelcome guest.

Teaching opportunities at:

TEXT Level
Reading comprehension

1 Ask the children to describe the setting of the story by reference to the illustration. Encourage them to use appropriate descriptive language, such as snug, cosy, comfortable, warm to describe the scene inside contrasting with the cold, icy, snowy scene outside.

2 Look at the title and ask the children why they think Owl might be standing at the door.

3 The story is one of contrasts – the cosy setting inside the treehouse compared with the weather outside (touched on in point 1), the peace and calm at the beginning compared with the havoc caused by Winter; the kindness of Owl compared with the rudeness of Winter. Read the story to the children and ask them to express their opinions of Owl and Winter and to use appropriate words to describe them.

4 Encourage the children to use their own adjectives to describe the tranquillity at the beginning of the story, and the trail of devastation created by Winter.

5 In what way is Winter like the Brute family in Unit 3.2? *(They are both thoughtless and selfish.)*

6 How do the children think the story will continue? Will Winter leave quietly? What else might it get up to? How will Owl get Winter out?

7 If possible, find and read some other extracts or stories by Arnold Lobel for the purpose of comparison (see Related texts)

Key Stage 1
Literacy Poster Pack 2

Letts
EDUCATIONAL

The Guest

Owl was at home.

"How good it feels to be sitting by this fire," said Owl. "It is so cold and snowy outside." Owl was eating buttered toast and hot pea soup for supper. Owl heard a loud sound at the front door. "Who is there, banging and pounding at my door on a night like this?" he said.

Owl opened the door. No one was there. Only the snow and the wind. Owl sat near the fire again. There was another loud noise at the door. "Who can it be," said Owl, "knocking and thumping at my door on a night like this?" Owl opened the door. No one was there. Only the snow and the cold. "The poor old winter is knocking at my door," said Owl. "Perhaps it wants to sit by the fire. Well I will be kind and let the winter come in."

Owl opened his door very wide. "Come in, Winter," said Owl. "Come in and warm yourself for a while."

Winter came into the house. It came in very fast. A cold wind pushed Owl against the wall. Winter ran around the room. It blew out the fire in the fireplace. The snow swirled up the stairs and whooshed down the hallway.

"Winter!" cried Owl. "You are my guest. This is no way to behave!"

But Winter did not listen. It made the curtains flap and shiver. It turned the pea soup into hard, green ice. Winter went into all the rooms in Owl's house. Soon everything was covered in snow.

"You must go, Winter!" shouted Owl. "Go away, right now!"

From The Guest by Arnold Lobel

© Letts Educational 1998   See *Letts Literacy Activity Book 2 Term 3* page 10

Writing comprehension

1 Ask the children to write a simple review of the story. Give them the following help: ask them to write the title and the name of the author; write about who was in the story and what they were like; write where the story took place; write something they liked about the story.

2 Winter was very bad-mannered. Ask the children to write five rules about how to behave well in someone else's house.

SENTENCE Level
Grammatical awareness

1 The story is full of action and emotions. Ask the children to read it aloud, with intonation and expression appropriate to the grammar and punctuation.

2 Revisit the work done on each character. Draw two columns on the board, one headed 'Owl' and the other 'Winter'. Brainstorm and ask the children to write words which describe each character in the correct column.

Sentence construction and punctuation

1 Owl said to Winter, 'This is no way to behave' (in other words, 'behave yourself'). Ask the children to think of different ways of asking for help, asking the time, asking someone to be quiet, etc. Think of some polite ways and some rude ways of doing it.

WORD Level
Spelling

1 Undertake a new word-making activity, starting with the word 'near' from the text. Ask the children to change the 'n' of 'near' to 'd', 'f', 'g', 'h', 'r', 't', 'y', 'cl' and 'app' and to write the new words they make. ('Dear', 'fear', 'gear', 'hear', 'rear', 'year', 'clear' and 'appear'.)

2 Ask the children to add a 'd' to the end of 'hear'. What happens? (It makes 'heard' and the pronunciation of the 'ea' changes.)

3 Write the word 'wear' on the board. Compare the difference in sound values of the 'ear' in 'wear' and 'near'. Make some more words. Change the 'w' of 'wear' to 'b', 'p', 't'. ('Bear', 'pear', 'tear'.) Note how 'tear' can be pronounced differently, depending on the context in which it appears.

Vocabulary extension

1 As the story is one of contrasts, do some work on antonyms (words with the opposite meaning). Choose some words from the story and ask the children to supply suitable words or phrases that mean the opposite.

Related texts

Other titles by Arnold Lobel:

'The Frog and Toad Pop-up Book
(There are other Frog and Toad books)

'Let's Talk About Being Rude' by Joy Wilt Berry (A story about good manners)

Playing With Words

About the text

Language is endlessly fascinating. It can be used for a variety of purposes, not least of which is using it purely for entertainment and enjoyment. This poster involves a number of rhymes, riddles and tongue twisters which do just that.

Teaching opportunities at:

TEXT Level
Reading comprehension

1 Read each tongue twister slowly to the children. Ask the children what they notice about many of the words in each. *(Alliteration – the use of the same letter or letters at the beginning of successive words – is an integral feature of all tongue twisters.)* Ask the children to read the tongue twisters slowly as well, and then to try speeding up. Do they know any more? If possible, find and read a selection of others, too. Ask the children to identify the common features in each.

2 Riddles have been around for centuries. (Jason in Greek mythology, had to solve riddles to find the Golden Fleece. The Vikings were inveterate riddlers, too!) The two riddles on the poster are of different types but both involve solving a puzzle. To solve the first riddle, logic needs to be applied. *(A cow.)* Read the second riddle and ask for suggestions of what it could be. *(A chair.)* Support the children when they are working it out. (The fact that it is a rhyming riddle should also be a big help.) Find, read and solve riddles from other sources. (Children's comics are often a good source.)

Key Stage 1
Literacy Poster Pack 2 — *Letts* EDUCATIONAL

Playing with Words

Tongue Twisters
Round and round the rugged rock the ragged rascal ran.

Swan swam over the sea –
Swim, swan, swim!
Swan swam back again –
Well swum swan!

Humorous Rhymes
The elephant carries a great big trunk,
But he never packs it with clothes;
It has no lock and has no key,
But he takes it wherever he goes.

One fine October morning
In September, last July,
The moon lay thick upon the ground,
The snow shone in the sky.
The flowers were singing merrily,
The birds were in full bloom,
I went down to the cellar
To sweep the upstairs room.

'What am I?' Riddles
My first is in CAT but not in DOG,
My second is in SNOW and also in FOG,
My last is in WHY and also in HOW,
My whole is an animal known as a _____.

I have four legs but cannot walk,
My back aches when you are comfortable.

© Letts Educational 1998   See *Letts Literacy Activity Book 2 Term 3*   page 12

3 Read the last two rhymes to the class and ask the children for their opinions of them. Point out the play on words in the first (playing on the fact that the word 'trunk' has two meanings). Ask the children what they think makes the second rhyme funny. Look for and read other humorous rhymes and poems (see Related texts). Encourage the children to practise them and read them aloud, too.

Writing comprehension

1 Encourage the children to make up their own alliterative tongue twisters.

2 After reading several more riddles, ask the children to work in pairs to try and make up some of their own. (The first type of riddle on the poster is easier than the second, which is a fairly sophisticated activity at this level.)

3 Suggest the children try making up some nonsense sentences (trying to rhyme them is probably asking too much at first). Reread the second rhyme and notice how the ideas are juxtaposed. Often opposite and contradictory ideas feature strongly. Give the children an example or two as starters, e.g. 'I went to bed last night yesterday morning'.

SENTENCE Level
Grammatical awareness

1 Provide the children with some sentences which don't make sense, such as 'The cat barked loudly and the dog purred'. Ask the children to rewrite these so the subjects and verbs agree.

Sentence construction and punctuation

1 Ask the children to make up lists of four or five alliterative words. Make sure they punctuate their lists correctly using commas, as with 'cling, clang, clink, clank and clunk' (see Vocabulary extension, point 1).

WORD Level
Spelling

1 Use rhyming as a theme to study and discuss words which have the same sounds but different letter patterns. Ask the children to supply as many words as possible that rhyme with a given word, say, 'head' and 'bed', 'red', 'said', etc. Then ask them to rewrite the resulting list of words in sets, according to common letter patterns.

Vocabulary extension

1 Ask the children to use a children's dictionary to look up words beginning with the same letter or groups of letters, e.g. consonant digraphs like 'sh' and 'ch', consonant blends like 'pr' and 'bl', and to use these as a basis for composing alliterative lists (see Sentence construction and punctuation point 1).

Related texts

'My First Has Gone Bonkers' by Brian Moses (These are fun poems and wordplay, etc.)

'The Nuttiest Riddle Book in the World' by Morrie Gallant

'Rhymes and Riddles' by Fran Pickering

'What Am I? Very First Riddles' by Stephanie Calmerson

'The Funniest Riddle Book in the World' by Morrie Gallant

Animal Language

About the text

This extract comes from the well-known Dr Dolittle book by Hugh Lofting. It is the part where the doctor learns to understand and speak the animals' language.

Teaching opportunities at:

TEXT Level
Reading comprehension

1 Look at the acknowledgement at the bottom of the poster. Ask the children which book this extract comes from and who wrote it. *(It is from 'The Story of Dr Dolittle' by Hugh Lofting.)* Discuss whether any of the children have read the book or seen the film. If so, encourage them to tell the others what they know about Dr Dolittle. Following this, ask them to look at the illustration and describe what is happening in it, and why they think the animals are waiting outside the doctor's home.

2 Read the story to and with the class. Encourage them to use phonological, contextual, grammatical and graphic knowledge to work out, predict and check the meanings of unfamiliar words and make sense of what they read.

3 Using the text, inference and imagination, ask the children to describe the setting of the story; the main character Doctor Dolittle (what he looks like, what sort of a man he is, what sort of things he does and says); and the plot (what the main events in the story are). *(Answers will depend on the children's interpretation.)*

4 Discuss the way the parrot says the dog 'talks'. Ask the children who have dogs how

Key Stage 1
Literacy Poster Pack 2
Letts EDUCATIONAL

Animal Language

At tea time, when the dog, Jip, came in, the parrot said to the Doctor, 'See, *he's* talking to you.'

'Looks to me as though he were scratching his ear,' said the Doctor.

'But animals don't always speak with their mouths,' said the parrot in a high voice, raising her eyebrows. 'They talk with their ears, with their feet, with their tails – with everything. Sometimes they don't *want* to make a noise. Do you see now the way he's twitching up one side of his nose?'

'What's that mean?' asked the Doctor.

'That means "Can't you see it's stopped raining?"' Polynesia answered. 'He is asking you a question. Dogs nearly always use their noses for asking questions.'

After a while, with the parrot's help, the Doctor got to learn the language of the animals so well that he could talk to them himself and understand everything they said. Then he gave up being a people's doctor altogether...

As soon as the other animals found out that he could talk their language they told him where the pain was and how they felt, and of course it was easy for him to cure them.

Now all these animals went back and told their brothers and friends that there was a doctor in the little house with the big garden that really was a doctor. And whenever any creatures got sick – not only horses and cows and dogs, but all the little things in the fields, like harvest mice and water voles, badgers and bats – they came at once to his house on the edge of the town, so that his big garden was nearly always crowded with animals trying to get in to see him.

From The Story of Doctor Dolittle by Hugh Lofting

© Letts Educational 1998   See *Letts Literacy Activity Book 2* Term 3   page 14

they know what their dog wants. How do they communicate? (If appropriate, this could lead on to a consideration of how we can 'talk' without our voices by using body language and gesture.)

5 Encourage the children to volunteer the titles of some stories in which animals talk like humans. You might like to remind them of Unit 3.3, 'The Guest'.

Writing comprehension

1 Ask the children to imagine and write about some very difficult animals that Dr Dolittle has to deal with. Some possible suggestions are 'an elephant who gets stuck in the door', 'the hippo who breaks the examination table' or 'the giraffe who gets his head stuck up the chimney'.

SENTENCE Level
Grammatical awareness

1 Provide the children with some simple sentences on the theme of animal noises, but with one verb missing. Children have to complete the missing verb, paying attention to necessary subject/verb agreement, so 'A dog barks but dogs _____' (bark).

Sentence construction and punctuation

1 Ask the children to make up some simple what, when, where, who and why questions for others to answer, based on the story extract.

WORD Level
Spelling

1 Choose a variety of words from the story, for instance 'badger', and ask the children to find smaller words hiding in the longer words. (In this case, 'bad' and 'badge'.)

Vocabulary extension

1 Brainstorm and collect as many different words as possible that describe animal noises, e.g. 'purr', 'moo', 'bark' and 'gobble', and animal movements, e.g. 'hop', 'slide', 'gallop' and 'lumber'.

Related texts

'"Stand Back," Said the Elephant, "I'm Going to Sneeze"' by Patricia Thomas and Wallace Tripp

Stories and poems:

'Tales from Wind in the Willows' by Kenneth Grahame

'Stories of Winnie-the-Pooh Together with Favourite Poems' by A. A. Milne

Winnie-the-Pooh

About the text

This poster features fascinating biographical detail about A. A. Milne, the author, and E. H. Shepard, the illustrator of the Winnie-the-Pooh stories and poems. It is taken from the cover of 'The Complete Collection of Winnie-the-Pooh' stories and poems.

Teaching opportunities at:

TEXT Level
Reading comprehension

1 Look at the title, illustration and introduction. Ask the children to volunteer what they know about Winnie-the-Pooh and to talk about any stories or poems they have read about him. Explain that this particular bear has been a well-known character for many years. Also tell the children that we can often learn a lot about authors and illustrators from book blurbs on the covers of books.

2 Read the text to the class. The actual text was written for adults so there are several potentially unfamiliar and tricky words in it. Encourage the children to use phonological, contextual, grammatical and graphic knowledge to work out, predict and check the meanings of these words and to make sense of what they read.

3 The blurb contains many fascinating facts, e.g. about who the characters were based on, where the adventures are set, etc. Ask the children to explain the things they learned which were of particular interest to them.

4 Do a simple sum and work out how many years the stories have been around.

Key Stage 1
Literacy Poster Pack 2

Letts EDUCATIONAL

Winnie-the-Pooh
Have you ever read any Winnie-the-Pooh stories or poems? This information about Winnie-the-Pooh, and the men who wrote and illustrated the books, was taken from the cover of this book.

Winnie-the-Pooh made his first appearance in a poem called 'Teddy Bear' by A. A. Milne, which appeared in *Punch* magazine, in 1923. A. A. Milne's verses were later published in the collection, *When We Were Very Young*, in 1924. The illustrator, E. H. Shepard, was an inspired choice, and the book quickly became a favourite with both young and adult readers.

When, in 1926, A. A. Milne's first stories about Winnie-the-Pooh were published, the book was an instant success. Since then, Winnie-the-Pooh has become a world-famous bear, with A. A. Milne's stories about Pooh and his forest friends translated into thirty-one different languages.

This beautiful edition contains the stories by A. A. Milne from *Winnie-the-Pooh* 1926, and *The House at Pooh Corner* 1928, and the poems from *When We Were Very Young* 1924, and *Now We Are Six* 1927.

The characters of Pooh, Piglet, Eeyore, Tigger, Kanga and Roo, are based upon the real nursery toys belonging to A. A. Milne's son, Christopher Robin, and their adventures are set in the Ashdown Forest where Milne and his family lived. The artist, E. H. Shepard, lovingly depicted the Forest and the toys in his drawings and the places he drew can still be seen today.

From Winnie-the-Pooh – The Complete Collection of Stories and Poems *by A. A. Milne*

© Letts Educational 1998   See *Letts Literacy Activity Book 2* Term 3 page 16

5 Encourage the children to ask people at home if they have read any A. A. Milne stories. Encourage them to ask their parents and relatives to suggest the names of other significant authors they remember from childhood.

6 Ask the children to suggest any names of authors (and possibly illustrators) they can remember. (Sometimes the author and illustrator are one and the same, as in the case of John Burningham, Unit 2.4.) As a routine, take time to note and discuss the authors of stories read to the class. Encourage the children to look at book blurbs and to find out more about significant authors. (Encyclopedias often have some basic information about popular writers.)

7 Find and read some other Winnie-the-Pooh stories and poems (see Related texts).

Writing comprehension

1 Encourage the children to make up some of their own Winnie-the-Pooh adventures. Use this as an opportunity to think more about the publishing process. Begin by brainstorming ideas and getting the children to draft their first version. Help them to edit and refine them and to produce a final draft. Think about its presentation – should it be hand-written or word-processed? Where will illustrations go? What is the title? Will it have covers with a book blurb and details about the author? Will it be part of an anthology of class stories? Will it be a concertina book, have stapled pages or be stuck onto sheets of coloured paper? Who will read it? Where will it be made available?

SENTENCE Level
Grammatical awareness

1 Choose some verbs from the story which have an irregular past tense, such as 'wrote – write', 'drew – draw', 'made – make', 'became – become' and 'was – is'. Use the formula, 'Today I write a story. Yesterday I _____ (wrote) a story'. Ask the children to supply the appropriate form of the verb. Extend this to other such verbs, such as 'catch', 'see' and 'go'.

Sentence construction and punctuation

1 Encourage the children to make up some questions of their own about the text using 'wh' words like 'who', 'where' and 'when'. This could be extended to making up questions they would like to ask the author or illustrator, or even Winnie-the Pooh-himself.

WORD Level
Spelling

1 Hold a 'letter pattern' hunt. Select some phonemes or letter patterns you would like the children to focus on, examples of which may be found in the passage. For example, 'all', 'our', 'oi', 'oo', 'cc' and 'ss'. Ask the children to find words containing these and to supply at least one other word they know which contains the same letter pattern. ('all': 'called'; 'our': 'favourite'; 'oi': 'choice'; 'oo': 'Pooh', 'books', 'Roo'; 'cc': 'success' and 'ss': 'success'.)

Vocabulary extension

1 After discussion, suggest the children write simple definitions for some of the less familiar words in the passage, perhaps words like 'instant' or 'translate'.

2 Use the blurb as an opportunity for suggesting and collecting words to do with books – the people who write them, the features of books themselves (covers, spines, contents, etc.) and the process of publishing.

Related texts

Other titles by A. A. Milne:

'Christopher Robin and Pooh Come to an Enchanted Place'

'Christopher Robin Gives Pooh a Party'

'The Christopher Robin Story Book'

'The Complete Winnie-the-Pooh'

The Jungle Book

About the text

This extract, from the famous Rudyard Kipling book, describes how Mowgli grew up and learned the ways of the jungle from his animal protectors and friends.

Teaching opportunities at:

TEXT Level
Reading comprehension

1 With the class, look at the title, illustration and name of the author. Ask if any of the children have read the book or seen the film version of the story. Encourage any who has to share their memories and opinions of either. Focus on the characters, setting and basic story line. Draw out the fact that Mowgli was 'adopted' by the animals and brought up by them in the jungle. Explain that this extract from the book tells a little about this process.

2 Read the passage to the class. Using the illustration, text and their imagination, ask the children to describe the setting in which Mowgli lives. Encourage children to use descriptive words and not be limited by the text itself.

3 Which characters does Mowgli have most contact with?

4 Ask the children to suggest the sorts of skills Mowgli might need to survive in the jungle. What dangers might he have to face?

5 Discuss with the children which of the stories about animals they have read this term they prefer, and why (refer back to Unit 3.3 'The Guest' and 3.5 'Animal Language').

6 Either carry out a search yourself, or encourage the children to look in an encyclopedia, to try to find out more about Rudyard Kipling.

Writing comprehension

1 Brainstorm some possible adventures Mowgli might have had. Provide a few, such as 'The day Mowgli … helped the bay elephant who was lost; … rescued the injured monkey; … faced a fierce tiger, etc.' as starters. Discuss and flesh out a few of these suggestions, writing key ideas, phrases and words on the board. Encourage the children to write their own sustained story using their knowledge of story elements gained, paying attention to settings, characterisation, story line, dialogue and appropriate story language.

Key Stage 1
Literacy Poster Pack 2
Letts EDUCATIONAL

The Jungle Book

This is the story of how the boy Mowgli was brought up in the jungle. When Mowgli was a baby, he was saved from a tiger and brought up by a pair of wolves, with help from Baloo, a sleepy old brown bear, and Bagheera, a black panther.

Mowgli grew up with the wolf cubs, though they, of course, were grown wolves almost before he was a child, and Father Wolf taught him his business, and the meaning of things in the Jungle, till every rustle in the grass, every breath of the warm night air, every note of the owls above his head, every scratch of a bat's claws as it roosted for a while in a tree, and every splash of every little fish jumping in a pool, meant just as much to him as the work of his office means to a business man. When he was not learning, Mowgli sat out in the sun and slept, and ate and went to sleep again; when he felt dirty or hot he swam in the forest pools; and when he wanted honey (Baloo told him that nuts and honey were just as pleasant to eat as raw meat) he climbed up for it, and that Bagheera showed him how to do it. Bagheera would lie out on a branch and call, 'Come along, Little Brother,' and at first Mowgli would cling like a sloth, but afterward he would fling himself through the branches almost as boldly as the grey ape. Mowgli took his place at the Council Rock, too, when the Pack met, and there he discovered that if he stared hard enough at any wolf, the wolf would be forced to drop his eyes, and so he used to stare for fun. At other times he would pluck the long thorns out of the pads of his friends, for wolves suffer terribly from thorns and burrs in their coats.

From The Jungle Book
by Rudyard Kipling

© Letts Educational 1998   See Letts Literacy Activity Book 2 Term 3   page 18

SENTENCE Level
Grammatical awareness

1 Mowgli had to learn to make sense of his new environment. Provide the children with either some sentences in which no spacing is left between the words, or sentences in which the words are in the wrong order or in which deliberate grammatical mistakes have been made. These sentences should be related in some way to the story. Ask the children to write them correctly.

Sentence construction and punctuation

1 Provide the children with some sentences based on the story which need punctuating. You might leave off capital letters at the beginning of the sentence and write people's names in lower case, and omit full stops, commas and question marks, etc. Ask the children to write them correctly.

WORD Level
Spelling

1 Use the text for a 'high frequency word' hunt. Select some words from the High Frequency Word List on pages 74–75, then ask the children to see how many they can find in the text.

2 Find and discuss words which have been suffixed in some way in the text, e.g. 'dirty', 'owls', 'jumping' and 'wanted'. Study each word and decide which root word it has grown from. *('Dirt', 'owl', 'jump' and 'want'.)*

Vocabulary extension

1 Ask the children to list some of the jungle animals mentioned in the story, and to add others they know about. Think of ways of categorising these, perhaps those that live in trees; on the ground; small or large animals; the way they move, and so on.

2 List some words from the text, e.g. 'warm', 'teach' and 'pleasant', and ask the children to suggest some synonyms (words or phrases with similar meanings) for each one you choose.

Related texts

The 'Just So Stories' by Rudyard Kipling

'A Nice Walk in the Jungle' by Nan Bodsworth

The Veterinary Surgeon

About the text

The poster features a page from a typical, age-appropriate information book on the topic of the job of a veterinary surgeon.

Teaching opportunities at:

TEXT Level
Reading comprehension

1 Ask how many children have pets. How many of them have ever been to the vets with their pets? Ask the children to explain what a vet is and the sort of thing he or she does. If they could interview a vet, what sort of questions would they like to ask him or her about their job? Ask the children to record some of these and check after reading the text if any have been answered.

2 Look at the title of the text. Explain that the word 'vet' is a shortened way of saying 'veterinary surgeon'. *('Veterinary' relates to animals and 'surgeon' meaning someone who performs operations, like a doctor.)*

3 Skim read the headings and sub-headings and glance at the illustrations to give the class an idea of the sorts of things the text is going to be about.

4 Scan the text to find specific paragraphs, for instance, where you would look to find out about the instruments a vet uses.

5 Close read the text with the class, relating the text to the illustrations whilst doing so.

6 Ask the children to list five facts they found interesting about the vet. Explain that a fact is something true, and that story books are called 'fiction', meaning they are made-up and not true. Explain that reference books like this are called 'non-fiction' books.

Key Stage 1
Literacy Poster Pack 2

Letts EDUCATIONAL

Veterinary Surgeon

Veterinary surgeon

I am a veterinary surgeon and I treat sick animals. I examine cats, dogs, and other small pets in my surgery. And if a cow or horse is unwell, I go by car to visit it on the farm. Then I give it medicine to make it well.

Difficult patients
Sometimes vets visit unusual patients in zoos. These animals may be too dangerous to treat when awake. Lions often have to be tranquillised first.

Vets visits
People carry their pets to surgery in baskets so they don't run away.

Vets' instruments
Vets' instruments help them treat sick animals. Animals must keep still and not bite. To stop a dog biting, the vet may use a muzzle.

muzzle / scissors / clippers / ear torch

At the farm
Vets may treat whole herds of cows. To stop them catching and spreading an illness, they may all be injected on one day.

At the surgery
Pets wait in the waiting room for the vet to see them.

A sick cat
During a check-up, the vet asks how the animal is behaving. He then examines the animal to find out what is wrong.

From Jobs People Do by Christopher Maynard

© Letts Educational 1998   **See Letts Literacy Activity Book 2 Term 3** page 20

7 Discuss how helpful the pictures were in understanding the text.

8 Point out that the introductory paragraph is really a summary of the job the vet does, and that each sub-section is an elaboration of some of the aspects of the vet's work.

Writing comprehension

1 Ask the children to write a simple sentence, using each sub-heading as the basis. For example, 'At the Farm – Vets visit farms and look after sick farm animals'. This is a simple way of making notes on the page of information, as each sub-heading summarises the main point of each paragraph. Give the sentences a title such as 'The work of a veterinary surgeon'.

2 Ask the children to write a similar non-fiction text on the work of, say, a nurse, a police officer or a firefighter. Base the writing on the structure and layout of the poster. Allow the children time to do any necessary research from information books first. Alternatively, this could be written more as a straight non-chronological report on the work of one of these people.

SENTENCE Level
Grammatical awareness

1 The first paragraph is written in the first-person. Ask the children to rewrite it replacing 'I' with 'the vet' and 'he' or 'she'. Note and discuss the difference this makes to the verbs.

Sentence construction and punctuation

1 Use the question-writing activity (Reading comprehension point 1) to encourage the children to frame and punctuate question writing appropriately.

WORD Level
Spelling

1 List some of the difficult words from the text, like 'veterinary', 'surgeon', 'examine', 'medicine', 'spreading', 'injected' and 'behaving'. Study each word one at a time. Are there any small words hiding in the longer words? Are there any common letter patterns or phonemes the children recognise? Are there any other words that are similar in any way? Has the word been prefixed or suffixed? Can the root word be identified? Can the word be broken down into smaller parts as an aid to spelling? Ask the children to underline any tricky bits as a reminder and a focus. Can they suggest other ways to remember them? *(Remind the children of the 'Look, say, cover, write, check' strategy.)*

Vocabulary extension

1 Choose a number of animals that a vet might come into contact with. Draw and label the parts of each animal (using reference books for information).

Related texts

See the 'A Day in the Life' series by Carol Watson, especially:

'A Day in the Life of a Nurse' (This series covers a wide range of occupations)

'Firefighter' by Alison Cooper

'Firefighters: A First Word and Picture Book' published by Campbell

'People's Jobs' by Paul Humphrey

'The Optician' by Rosalind Lenga

Using an Information Book

About the text

This poster shows three parts of an information book on cats – the contents page, index and glossary. This provides an ideal opportunity for focusing on, and learning about, these important features of information books.

Teaching opportunities at:

TEXT Level
Reading comprehension

1 Select a few information books from your library. Look at the covers and titles. Ask the children what they think each book is going to be about. Discuss the difference between fiction and non-fiction books.

2 Look at the poster and explain that this shows some helpful features of information books. Understanding them and knowing how to use them will help children be able to use the books more effectively.

3 Look first at the contents page and discuss what its purpose is. Ask some specific questions about the book based on the contents page shown on the poster.

4 Follow this up by turning to the contents pages of the school books to reinforce the points made on the poster.

5 Follow the same procedure for dealing with the index, talking about its purpose, where it may be located and the fact that it is in alphabetical order. Follow this up by reference to the school books.

6 Carry out the same type of activities for the glossary. (Do note that whilst most reference books will have a contents and an index, not all will have a glossary.)

Key Stage 1
Literacy Poster Pack 2
Letts EDUCATIONAL

Using an Information Book

Here are parts of three pages from an information book on cats. Knowing how to use these pages will help you a great deal.

Contents
Wild ones	2
The cat for you	4
Where to find your cat	6
A healthy cat – what to look for	8
Safe hands	10
Feeding time	12
Home sweet home	14
Keeping clean	16
At the vet's	18
No more kittens	20
A note from the RSPCA	22
Further reading	22
Glossary	23
Index	24

A contents page tells you what sections the book is divided into. It comes at the beginning of a book.

Index
C	cleaning 16
F	feeding 12, 13
	fleas 17
H	healthy 8, 13
K	keeping clean 4, 5
	kittens 20, 21
L	long-haired 4
P	playing 9
S	short-haired 4, 5
	sleeping 14, 15
V	vet 7, 17, 18, 19
W	wild cat 2

Glossary
grooming *brushing and combing your cat*
injections *cats have to be vaccinated/injected by a vet to stop them catching diseases.*
litter *new born kittens*

A glossary tells you the meaning of hard words. It comes near the end of a book.

An index tells you where to find specific things. It comes near the end of the book.

From Cats by Michaela Miller

© Letts Educational 1998   See Letts Literacy Activity Book 2 Term 3 page 22

---

7 Use the poster and the school books to draw attention to book blurbs, details of authors, publishers, etc.

Writing comprehension

1 Ask the children to write a review of an information book they have recently read or used. Encourage them to list the title, the author and the publisher; to include what the book was about; how readable or interesting it was (mentioning a few things they found of particular interest); how well illustrated it was; how useful the contents and index pages were; and whether it had a glossary.

SENTENCE Level
Grammatical awareness

1 Write a few sentences about a cat, such as 'My cat is brown. It has long whiskers and a long tail.' Ask the children to rewrite this as if you had two cats, so 'My cats are brown. They have long whiskers and tails.' Compare and discuss the differences.

Sentence construction and punctuation

1 Use information from the index on the poster, and indexes from other books, to write lists punctuated correctly with commas. For example, 'The book on cats contains information on cleaning, feeding, fleas, keeping clean and kittens.'

WORD Level
Spelling

1 Use the poster as an opportunity to secure phonemic spelling from the previous five terms. Identify phonemes to be focused on like 'oo'. Ask the children to find an example of a word containing the phoneme on the poster. ('Book', 'look' and 'grooming'.) Carry out a variety of activities reinforcing the phoneme by – changing the 'gr' in 'groom' to 'l', 'r', 'br' and 'gl' ('loom', 'room', 'broom', 'gloom'); thinking of other rhyming words; and thinking of other phonemes with the same sound but different spellings.

Vocabulary extension

1 Use a text the children are currently working on and choose some difficult or unfamiliar words from it. Make a glossary for the text, using the glossary on the poster as a model.

2 Give the children a list of topic words about animals or pets for them to sort into alphabetical order, according to the first letter.

Related texts

'The Kingfisher Book of 1001 Questions and Answers' by Bridget and Neil Ardley

'Children's Picture Encyclopedia' published by Dorling Kindersley

The Silly Ghosts Gruff

About the text

This story by Michael Rosen is, as the title suggests, a humorous parody of the traditional tale.

Teaching opportunities at:

TEXT Level
Reading comprehension

1 Ask the children if they have read, or know, the story of 'The Three Billy Goats Gruff'. Ask them to tell it in their own words.

2 Show children the title of the story on the poster and explain that it is a funny version of the same story but with some differences.

3 Read the story straight through to the class and ask for their immediate responses to it. Did they enjoy it? Did they find it funny? Ask them to justify their views and opinions and give their reasons. Which story do they like best – the original or this one?

4 Read the story through again. This time stop at these key places: when characters are introduced, ask who each character reminds them of. How does the way their names are written make them smile? Whenever there are changes in the setting from the traditional tale, follow the same line of questioning, e.g. the 'fridge' for the 'bridge'. Whenever word play is used, compare it with the original story, e.g. 'drip, drop, drip, drop' as opposed to 'trip, trap, trip, trap', and so on.

5 Ask: Is the basic story structure, sequence of events and ending the same as in the original?

6 Identify and draw the children's attention to typical story language, such as 'Once there were', 'And from that day on', etc., and common linking words or phrases such as 'Then along came' and 'Now'.

7 Find, read and discuss other stories and poems by Michael Rosen (see Related texts).

Writing comprehension

1 Writing parodies like this is very difficult. One way into it is to use simple nursery rhymes like 'Humpty Dumpty' and play with the names, words and story line. So 'Dumpy Humphrey was not very tall, so Dumpy Humphrey stood on a wall. Along came some women, along came some men, and told Dumpy Humphrey to get down again'. This may best be done as a collective class activity.

Key Stage 1
Literacy Poster Pack 2
Letts EDUCATIONAL

The Silly Ghosts Gruff

Once there were three ghosts. They were called the Silly Ghosts Gruff. There was Little Silly Ghost Gruff, Big Silly Ghost Gruff and Piddle-sized Silly Ghost Gruff. And they all lived in a field by a river. One day they thought they would like to cross the river to eat the grass on the other side.

Now, over this river there was a fridge and underneath this fridge was a horrible roll. A horrible Cheese roll. So the Little Silly Ghost Gruff, he stepped on the fridge, drip, drop, drip, drop, over the fridge; when suddenly, there on the fridge was the horrible roll.

'I'm a roll-foll-de-roll and you'll eat me up for your supper!'

'Oh no, oh no, oh no,' said Little Silly Ghost Gruff. 'I don't want to eat you. My big brother the Piddle-sized Silly Ghost Gruff is going to be coming along soon and he can eat you for his supper.'

'Very well,' said the horrible roll, 'you can cross the fridge.' And drip, drop, drip, drop, over the fridge went the Little Silly Ghost Gruff.

Exactly the same thing happened to the Piddle-sized Silly Ghost Gruff. Then along comes the Big Silly Ghost Gruff. Drip, drop, drip, drop, over the fridge, and, suddenly, there was the horrible roll again.

'I'm a roll-foll-de-roll and you'll eat me up for your supper!'

'Oh can I? Oh can I?' said the Big Silly Ghost Gruff. And at that he ran at the horrible roll and went straight through it (he was a ghost, don't forget). And so over the fridge he went drip, drop, drip, drop, till he got to the other side.

And from that day on, no roll, no cheese roll, or ham roll or even jam roll ever bothered the Silly Ghosts Gruff again.

The Silly Ghosts Gruff (slightly adapted) from Hairy Tales and Nursery Crimes by Michael Rosen

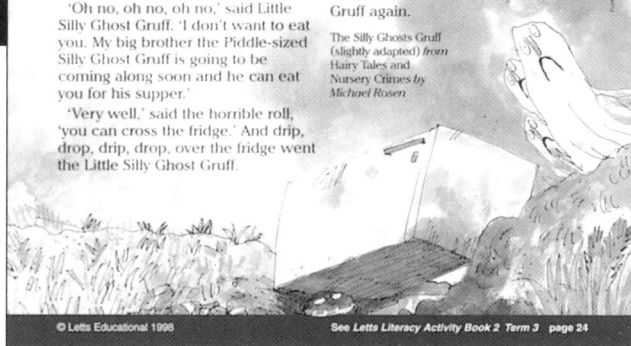

© Letts Educational 1998   *See Letts Literacy Activity Book 2 Term 3 page 24*

SENTENCE Level
Grammatical awareness

1 'Doctor' some well-known rhymes so they do not make sense. Ask the children to rewrite them sensibly, for instance, 'Little Tommy Horner fell in the corner, drinking his Christmas pie. He pulled out his thumb and put in a plum and said, "What a good girl am I." '

Sentence construction and punctuation

1 Find and write the names of the characters from the story, ensuring they begin with capital letters. Ask the children to write correctly the names of other storybook characters. (Note, too, the use of capital letters in book titles.)

WORD Level
Spelling

1 Use the words 'suddenly' and 'exactly' from the text as a focus. Break the words into root word plus suffix, e.g. 'sudden + ly = suddenly'. (Stress that the ending is always spelt '-ly' and not 'ley' – a common mistake many children make.) Look for other '-ly' adverbs in reading books and ask the children to carry out the same exercise. (It may be best to keep this simply to words in which the spelling of the root word does not change, as in the examples given. However, if appropriate, this activity could lead on to words ending in '-y' where the '-y' changes to 'i' before adding the ending, as with 'busy' – 'busily'.)

Vocabulary extension

1 Select some words from the text and ask the children to think of some synonyms (words with a similar meaning), e.g. 'horrible' – 'nasty', 'terrible' and 'awful', and antonyms (words with opposite meanings), e.g. 'pleasant', 'nice' and 'delightful'.

Related texts

'Moving' by Michael Rosen and Sophie Williams

'Quick, Let's Get Out of Here!' by Michael Rosen and Quentin Blake

'Wouldn't You Like to Know' by Michael Rosen

'When Did You Last Wash Your Feet?' by Michael Rosen

'Walking the Bridge of Your Nose' selected by Michael Rosen and Chloë Cheese

'Each Peach Pear Plum' by Janet and Allan Ahlberg

'Animal Nursery Rhymes' published by Dorling Kindersley

'Favourite Nursery Rhymes' by Jonathon Langley

'Jack and Jill: A Book of Nursery Rhymes' by Gwenda Beed Davey

High frequency word list

about	girl	may	sister
after	good	more	so
again	got	much	some
an		must	
another	had		take
as	half	name	than
	has	new	that
back	have	next	their
ball	help	night	them
be	her	not	then
because	here	now	there
bed	him		these
been	his	off	three
boy	home	old	time
brother	house	once	too
but	how	one	took
by		or	tree
	if	our	two
call(ed)		out	
came	jump	over	us
can't	just		
could		people	very
	last	pull	
did	laugh	push	want
dig	little	put	water
do	live(d)		way
don't	love	ran	were
door			what
down	made	saw	when
	make	school	where
first	man	seen	who
from	many	should	will
			with
			would
			your

Handy Hints for Learning to Spell New Words

Days of the week:
Sunday
Monday
Tuesday
Wednesday
Thursday
Friday
Saturday

Months of the year:
January
February
March
April
May
June
July
August
September
October
November
December

Common colour words:
black
white
blue
red
green
yellow
pink
purple
orange
brown

Numbers to 20:
one
two
three
four
five
six
seven
eight
nine
ten
eleven
twelve
thirteen
fourteen
fifteen
sixteen
seventeen
eighteen
nineteen
twenty

LOOK
- Look carefully at the word.
- Does it contain any letter patterns you already know?
- Do you know any other words like it?
- Which is the most difficult part of the word?
- Do you know what the word means?

SAY
- Say the word to hear how it sounds.
- Is the word spelled as it sounds?
- Can you break the word into smaller parts?

COVER
- Cover the word and try to see it in your mind.

WRITE
- Write the word from memory.
- Try not to copy.

CHECK
- Check your spelling with the original.
- Compare them.
- If you got it wrong, try it again.

Handy Hints for Planning Stories

SETTING

- Where will your story take place?
  - in a house?
  - in a shop?
  - in a wood?
  - in a castle?
  - in a hospital?
  - in a cave?
  - at the seaside?
  - at school?
  - at a fair?
  - somewhere else?

CHARACTERS

- Who will be in your story?
  - will they be humans?
  - will they be animals?
  - will they be monsters?
  - will they be something else?
- What will they look like?
- What sort of things will they do?
- What sort of things will they say?

STORYLINE

- What will your story be about?
- How will it begin?
- What sort of things will happen in the middle?
- How will your story end?
  - happily?
  - sadly?
  - amusingly?
  - will you make it into a 'cliffhanger', leaving the reader wanting to know more?

Handy Hints for Checking Your Writing

SENTENCES
- Do your sentences make sense?
- Is there anything you want to move or change?
- Is there anything you can leave out to make it clearer?

PUNCTUATION
- Have you punctuated it correctly with:
  - capital letters, full stops, question marks, exclamation marks, speech marks and commas?

SPELLING
- Have you checked for silly spelling mistakes?
- Have you looked up any words you are not sure of?

HANDWRITING
- Is your handwriting easy to read?
- Or are you going to do your work on the computer?

PRESENTATION
- Have you thought of a good title?
- Are you going to illustrate your work?
  - what sort of illustrations would be best? (pictures, diagrams, etc.)
  - where will you place the illustrations?
- In what form will you present your work?
  - in an exercise book?
  - on paper?
  - as a zig-zag concertina book?
  - in some other format?

Handy Hints for Handwriting

BEFORE YOU BEGIN

- Are you sitting comfortably?
- Are you sitting up straight?
- Have you got enough light?
- Have you got a smooth surface to write on?
- Have you sloped your paper slightly?
- Have you got a suitable pen or pencil to write with?
- Are you holding your pen or pencil in a comfortable way?
- Can you see what you are writing?

WHEN YOU HAVE FINISHED

- Is the writing neat?
- Is it easy to read?
- Does it 'sit' on the line?
- Are all letters well shaped?
- Are the letters evenly sized?
- Are any letters too tall or too small?
- Are the descenders of any letters too long or curly?
- Is there enough space between the words and letters?
- Are all the joins well made?
- Have you put capital letters in all the correct places?
- Have you used punctuation marks correctly?

Handy Hints for Using Punctuation Marks (1)

Punctuation helps us make sense of what we read.
Punctuation marks make writing easier for us to understand.
They help us to read with expression.

Full stop
A **full stop** tells you to stop. You have come to the end of a sentence.
Every sentence must begin with a capital letter.
The dog chased the postman.

Question mark
A **question mark** tells you a question is being asked.
What is the time?

Comma
A **comma** tells you to pause. It is also used to separate items in a list.
After eating his dinner, the old man had a sleep.
Mrs Jones had apples, pears, bananas and grapes in her bag.

Exclamation mark
An exclamation mark is used when we feel strongly about something or are surprised.
Stop that thief!

Speech marks
We use **speech marks** to show someone is speaking.
We write what the person says inside the speech marks.
Tom said, "I like to watch television in the evening."

Handy Hints for Using Punctuation Marks (2)

Apostrophe

An **apostrophe** is like a raised comma. It is used in two ways:

1. In **contractions** (when words are shortened by leaving out letters). The apostrophe shows something has been missed out.

For example, **do not** can be written as **don't**

2. It can be used to show **possession**.

– the book belonging to the girl = **the girl's book**

– the book belonging to the girls = **the girls' book**

Colon

A **colon** is often used to introduce a list, before someone speaks, or instead of a full stop.

He was very cold**:** the temperature was below zero.

The fridge contained**:** eggs, butter, milk and yoghurt.

Louise said**:** "What are you doing here?"

Semi-colon

A **semi-colon** is a punctuation mark used to separate parts of a sentence. It is stronger than a comma but not as strong as a full stop.

Sam loves Indian food**;** Tom prefers Italian food.

Dash

A **dash** holds words apart. It is stronger than a comma, but not as strong as a full stop.

There is only one meal worth eating **–** spaghetti!

Hyphen

Hyphens link words together.   I love freshly-baked bread.

Brackets

Brackets can be used like dashes. They can separate off part of a sentence or put in an extra example:

He was awarded a prize in school **(**not before time**)**

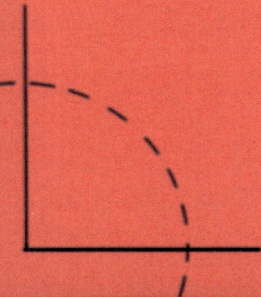

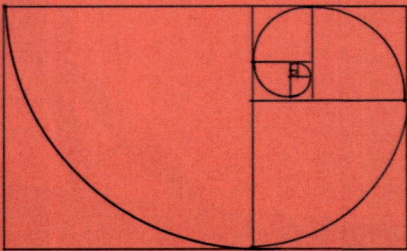

MATH MARVELS:

30 Cool facts to *WOW* your Brain!

Written by
Taarun Krushanth

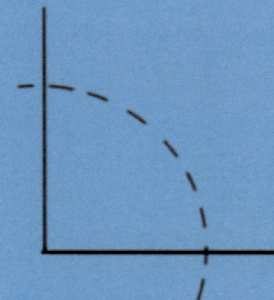

HI...

I'm Math kid!

I'm 6 years old! At the time this book was published, anyway.

I know what you're thinking... I'm too young to write a book about Math.

It might surprise you to know that right now I'm learning Statistics and Probability and from there... who knows!

I **LOVE** math! It's more or less all I talk about.

Sooooooo.... I thought why not write down some interesting math for other kids to inspire their math journey.

I might even inspire some grown-ups like....

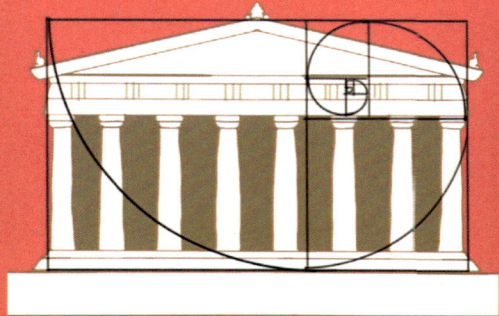

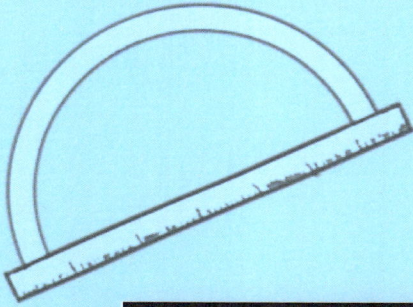

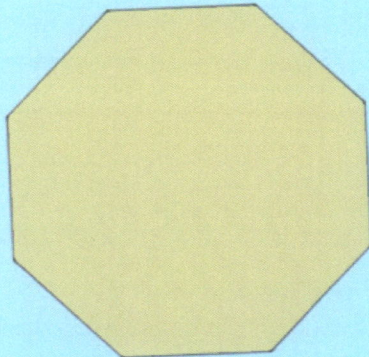

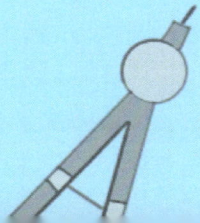

#1

Math in Everyday Life

Time for Math

12 1 2 3 4 5 6 7 8 9 10 11

Let's dive deep into some examples of how we use math in everyday life:

Playing Games: When you play board games like Monopoly or card games like Uno, you count the spaces you move or the points you score. In sports, you keep track of scores to see who's winning. For example, in soccer, you count how many goals each team has.

Shopping: When you go shopping, you use math to add up the prices of the items you want to buy. You also use math to calculate discounts. For example, if a toy is 20% off, you can figure out how much money you save.

At the cash register, you check if you have enough money to pay and calculate the change you'll get back.

Cooking and Baking: Recipes use measurements like cups, teaspoons, and grams. If a recipe says you need 2 cups of flour, you measure it out to get the right amount. Sometimes, you need to double a recipe or cut it in half. Math helps you figure out how much of each ingredient you need.

Traveling: When going on a trip, you might use math to calculate how long it will take to get there. If you're riding a bike or walking, you might measure the distance and figure out the best route.

Telling Time: You use math to read the clock and figure out how many minutes until your favourite TV show starts or how long you have to finish your homework.

Understanding time also helps you manage your day, like knowing when to leave for school or how long you can play before bedtime.

MATH HELPS US UNDERSTAND THE WORLD AROUND US AND MAKE DECISIONS. IT'S LIKE A SUPERPOWER WE USE EVERYDAY!

LET'S BAKE SOMETHING!

Math & Science

Let's explore how math and science work together like best friends to help us understand the world.

Math Helps Science

Math is like a toolbox for scientists. When scientists want to understand how things work, they use math to measure, calculate, and make sense of what they find.

Measuring and Counting: If a scientist wants to know how tall a tree is, they measure it using numbers. If they want to know how many birds live in a forest, they count them.

Experiments: Scientists do experiments to test ideas. They use math to collect data (like how fast something moves or how much something weighs) and figure out what it means.

Making Predictions: Scientists use math to make predictions. If they know how fast a rocket travels, they can calculate when it will reach space.

Science Helps Math

Science helps math by giving it real-world problems to solve. Without science, math would just be a bunch of numbers and rules without a purpose.

Physics and Math: Physics is a science that studies how things move and work. It uses a lot of math. For example, math helps physicists understand gravity, which is why we stay on the ground and don't float away.

Biology and Math: Biology is the study of living things. Math helps biologists understand things like how fast plants grow, how many animals live in a certain area, or how diseases spread.

Medicine: Doctors and scientists use math to figure out the right amount of medicine to give to patients. They also use math to study how diseases spread and find ways to stop them.

#2

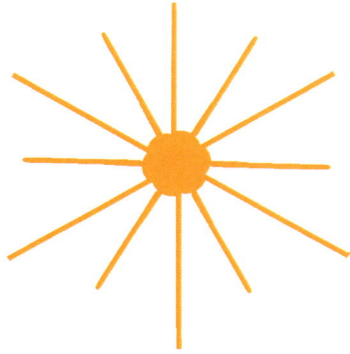

Meteorologists, who study weather, use math to predict if it will rain, snow, or be sunny. They measure temperature, wind speed, and more to make accurate forecasts.

Fun with Math and Science

Think about baking cookies again. Science explains how ingredients like baking powder make the dough rise, and math helps you measure the right amounts so your cookies turn out delicious. By working together, math and science make baking fun and tasty!

So, math and science are like best friends that help each other understand the world. Math gives science the tools to measure and predict, and science gives math real-world problems to solve. Together, they make amazing discoveries and help us in our everyday lives!

SCIENTISTS USE MATH TO CALCULATE THE PATH OF ROCKETS AND SATELLITES. WITHOUT MATH, WE COULDN'T SEND ASTRONAUTS TO THE MOON OR EXPLORE MARS.

#3

The Pythagoras theorem states that the square of the length of the hypotenuse is equal to the sum of squares of the lengths of other two sides of the right-angled triangle.

LET'S THINK

Two Dimensions (Flat Surface)

Imagine you have a big piece of paper. You draw a right-angle triangle on it, which is a triangle with one corner that is perfect square corner (like the corner of a book). If you know the lengths of the two shorter sides of the triangle, you ca find out how long the longest side (called the hypotenuse) is

THE RULE IS:

{Longest side}^{2} = {One side}^{2} + {Other side}^{2}

So, if one side is 3 units long and the other is 4 units long, you do

$$3^2 + 4^2 = 9^2 + 16 = 25$$

Then, the longest side is:

$$\sqrt{25} = 5$$

ABOUT IT LIKE THIS:

Three Dimensions (Space)

Now, imagine you are building something with blocks. You want to find out the distance from one corner of a box to the opposite corner, going through the inside of the box. This box has three sides: length, width, and height. The rule for the distance across the box is:

$$\text{Distance}^2 = \text{Length}^2 + \text{Width}^2 + \text{Height}^2$$

So, if the box is 3 units long, 4 units wide, and 5 units tall, you do:

$$3^2 + 4^2 + 5^2 = 9 + 16 + 25 = 50$$

Then, the distance across the box is:

$$\sqrt{50} = \text{approx. } 7.1$$

Higher Dimensions (More Complicated Spaces)

Imagine you have even more directions to move in, like a super complicated video game with many levels. The same kind of rule works to find distances. You just add up the squares of all the sides you are interested in.

So, in any number of dimensions, if you know the lengths of the sides, you can find the distance by using the same idea: add up the squares of the lengths of the sides, and then take the square root to find the distance.

IT'S LIKE MAGIC, BUT IT'S REALLY JUST MATH THAT WORKS IN EVERY KIND OF SPACE!

Exponential Growth

Let's explore exponential growth using a fun story about grains of rice and a chessboard.

#4

The Chessboard and the Grains of Rice

Imagine you have a chessboard. A chessboard has 64 squares (8 rows and 8 columns). Now, let's play a game with grains of rice:

Start with One Grain of Rice:

Place one grain of rice on the first square.

Double the Rice on Each Square:

On the second square, place two grains of rice.

On the third square, place four grains of rice.

On the fourth square, place eight grains of rice.

Each time you move to the next square, you double the number of grains of rice from the previous square.

WHAT HAPPENS NEXT?

Let's see how the number of grains grows:

1st square: 1 grain

2nd square: 2 grains (1 x 2)

3rd square: 4 grains (2 x 2)

4th square: 8 grains (4 x 2)

5th square: 16 grains (8 x 2)

As you keep going, the number of grains on each square gets very big, very fast.

Exponential Growth

This kind of growth, where you keep doubling, is called exponential growth. It means things grow really, really fast.

Why is it Amazing?

Let's see how many grains are on some of the later squares:

10th square: 512 grains

20th square: 524,288 grains

30th square: 536,870,912 grains

By the time you get to the 64th square, the number of grains of rice is so huge, it's hard to imagine!

Why It's Important

Exponential growth shows how quickly things can add up when they keep doubling. It's like magi

Real-Life Examples

Populations:

If bacteria multiply by splitting into two every hour, their numbers grow very fast, just like the grains of rice.

Computers:

Computer speeds and storage capacities have grown exponentially over the years, meaning they've gotten much faster and can hold a lot more information very quickly.

Fun Fact

If you actually placed all those grains of rice on the chessboard, you'd end up with more rice than there is in the entire world! That's how powerful exponential growth is.

So next time you see something growing very quickly, remember the story of the rice and the chessboard. It helps us understand why things that grow exponentially can get very big, very fast!

10,000,000,000,000,
000,000,000,000,00
0,000,000,000,000,
000,000,000,000,00
0,000,000,000,000,
000,000,000,000,00
0,000,000,000,000,
000,000,000,000

Googology is the study of large numbers

Have you ever wondered how big numbers can get? Like, REALLY big numbers? Well, that's what Googology is all about! Googology is the study of really big numbers. These numbers are so huge that they make your head spin just thinking about them!

Where Did It Start?

It all started with a number called a "googol." A googol is a 1 followed by 100 zeros. That's a lot of zeros! Here's what a googol looks like:

**10,000,000,000,000,0
00,000,000,000,000,
000,000,000,000,000
,000,000,000,000,00
0,000,000,000,000,0
00,000,000,000,000,
000,000,000,000,000
,000,000**

Can you imagine counting to that number? It would take forever!

The name "googol" was actually made up by a 9-year-old boy named Milton Sirotta in 1938. Pretty cool, right?

Even Bigger Numbers

If you think a googol is big, wait until you hear about a googolplex! A googolplex is a 1 followed by a googol zeros. That's like trying to write a googol of zeros! It's so big that if you tried to write it out, there wouldn't be enough space in the entire universe to fit all the zeros!

Why Do We Study Big Numbers?

You might wonder, "Why do we need such big numbers?" Well, studying big numbers helps mathematicians and scientists understand the limits of what we can count and measure. It also helps them think about really large concepts in science, like the size of the universe or the number of possible chess games.

Graham's Number

One of the biggest numbers ever used in a serious math problem is called Graham's number. It's so gigantic that even if you wrote it out, your brain wouldn't be able to comprehend it. Instead of writing it down, mathematicians use special notation to describe it. It's so big that if you tried to think about it, your head might feel like it's going to explode!

Playing with Big Numbers

You can have fun with big numbers too! Try making up your own super huge number and give it a funny name. Maybe you could invent the "tenyojillion" or the "gigantosaur." The possibilities are endless!

Wrapping Up

So, next time you think about numbers, remember that they can get unimaginably big. Googology is like a playground for numbers, where they can grow as large as your imagination can take them. Who knows? Maybe you'll be the next person to come up with an even bigger number!

#6 INFINITY

∞

Infinity is a concept that describes something that never ends.

Imagine the biggest number you can think of. Got it? Now, add one to it. You can always add one more, right? No matter how big the number is, there's always a number bigger than it. That's infinity! It's like a never-ending adventure with numbers.

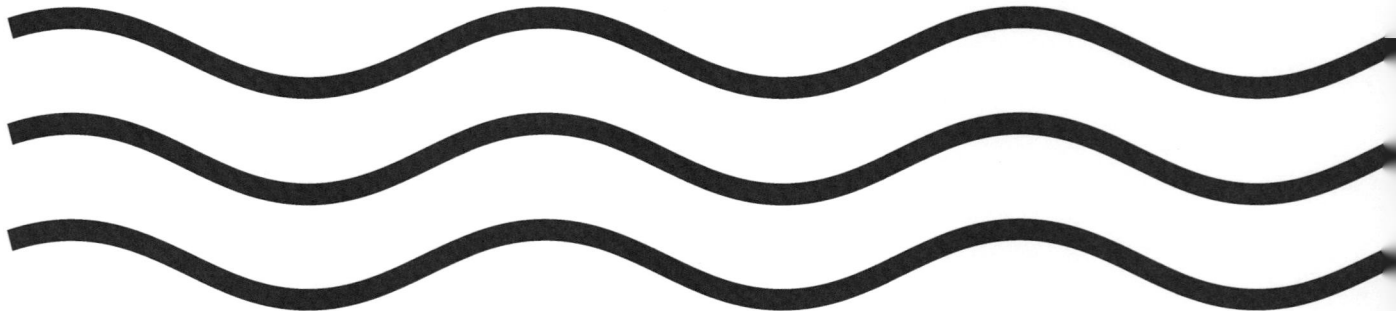

Here's a fun way to think about it: Picture a giant cookie jar. No matter how many cookies you take out, there are always more cookies inside. The jar never runs out of cookies. That's what infinity is like with numbers—they never run out!

Infinity is a special kind of number because it's not really a number you can count to. It's more like an idea that helps us understand things that go on forever. For example, the number of stars in the sky, the grains of sand on a beach, or even the time you could spend counting numbers.

So, infinity is a super cool concept because it reminds us that some things are just too big to measure, and the possibilities are endless!

Did you know there are different types of infinity?

It might sound surprising, but not all infinities are the same size. Let's explore this idea with a simple story.

Imagine you have two friends, Alice and Bob. Alice loves to count whole numbers (1, 2, 3, 4, ...), and Bob loves to count even numbers (2, 4, 6, 8, ...)

Alice's Infinity:

Alice starts counting: 1, 2, 3, 4, and so on. She will keep counting forever because there are infinitely many whole numbers.

Bob's Infinity:

Bob starts counting even numbers: 2, 4, 6, 8, and so on. He also will keep counting forever because there are infinitely many even numbers.

Now, you might think that both Alice and Bob have the same amount of numbers to count, right? They both have infinity. But here's the interesting part: mathematicians have discovered that some infinities are actually larger than others!

Bigger Infinity:

To see a bigger infinity, let's think about all the numbers between 0 and 1. These include 0.1, 0.12, 0.123, 0.1234, and so on. You can keep adding more and more digits after the decimal point, and there are infinitely many possible numbers between 0 and 1.

So, we have:

- Alice's whole numbers: 1, 2, 3, 4, ...

- Bob's even numbers: 2, 4, 6, 8, ...

- And all the tiny numbers between 0 and 1: 0.1, 0.12, 0.123, 0.1234, ...

There are actually more numbers between 0 and 1 than there are whole numbers or even numbers. This means that the infinity of numbers between 0 and 1 is a "bigger" infinity than the infinity of whole numbers or even numbers.

Prime Numbers

Let's talk about prime numbers in a fun and simple way.

Imagine you have a box of toys. Some toys can be grouped in many different ways, but some can only be grouped in one special way. Prime numbers are like those special toys that can only be grouped in one particular way.

Here's how it works:

A prime number is a number that can only be divided evenly by 1 and itself.

This means that when you try to split a prime number into equal groups, the only groups you can make are just one big group of the whole number or individual groups of 1.

The number 2 is a prime number. You can only divide it into 2 (2 divided by 2 equals 1) and 1 (2 divided by 1 equals 2). No other numbers work.

The number 3 is also a prime number. You can only divide it into 3 (3 divided by 3 equals 1) and 1 (3 divided by 1 equals 3).

Other examples of prime numbers are 5, 7, 11, and 13. These numbers can only be divided evenly by 1 and themselves.

#7

Why are Prime Numbers Special?

Prime numbers are like the building blocks of all numbers. Just like you can use blocks to build many things, you can use prime numbers to create other numbers.

- For example, you can multiply the prime numbers 2 and 3 to get 6. Or you can multiply 2, 2, and 3 to get 12.

Not Prime Numbers

Some numbers are not prime because you can split them into different equal groups. For example, 4 is not a prime number because you can divide it by 1, 2, and 4. (4 divided by 2 equals 2).

The number 6 is also not a prime number because you can divide it by 1, 2, 3, and 6.

In summary, prime numbers are special numbers that can only be split into one big group of the whole number or individual groups of 1. They are like the unique toys in your box that can only be grouped in one special way.

Fermat's Last Theorem

#8

Imagine you have a big puzzle with numbers, like a jigsaw puzzle but with numbers instead of pictures. Fermat's Last Theorem is about a very specific type of number puzzle.

Here's what the theorem says:

When you learn math, you often see equations like $a^2 + b^2 = c^2$. This means you add two squares of numbers to get another square. For example, $3^2 + 4^2 = 5^2$ because $9 + 16 = 25$.

Fermat's Last Theorem says that if you change the equation to use powers higher than 2, like $a^3 + b^3 = c^3$ or $a^4 + b^4 = c^4$, then there are no whole numbers (positive numbers like 1, 2, 3, etc.) that can make the equation true.

In other words, if you try to find three whole numbers a, b, and c that fit this new equation, you won't be able to.

This might seem simple, but proving it was really, really hard. Mathematicians tried to solve this puzzle for over 350 years!

A mathematician named Andrew Wiles finally solved it in 1994. He worked on this puzzle for many years and used a lot of very advanced math to prove that Fermat was right.

So, Fermat's Last Theorem is like a very tricky puzzle with numbers that says, "If you try to add two cubes (or higher powers) of numbers to get another cube (or higher power), you can't do it with whole numbers." And it took a very long time for someone to solve this puzzle!

The Adventure of Geometry

Geometry is the study of shapes, sizes, and spaces. It's like going on an adventure to explore the world of forms and figures.

Geometry is the study of shapes, sizes, and spaces. It's like going on an adventure to explore the world of forms and figures.

Angles can be:

Right angle: 90 degrees, like the corner of a square.

Acute angle: Less than 90 degrees, like a sharp corner.

Obtuse angle: More than 90 degrees, like a wide corner.

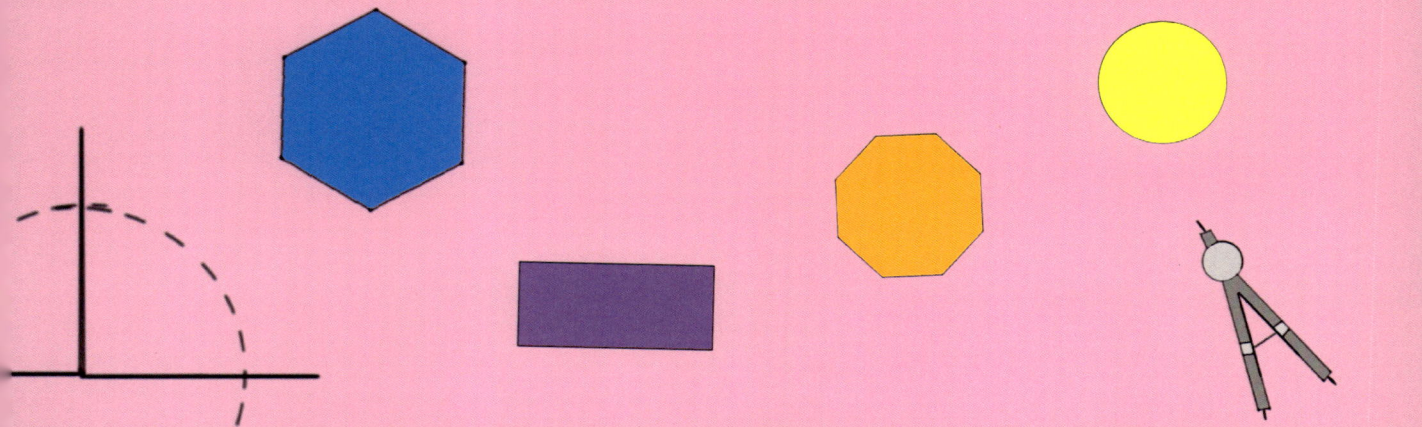

Perimeter and Area

Geometry helps us measure things. The perimeter is the distance around a shape. For a rectangle, add up all the sides. The area is the space inside a shape. For a rectangle, multiply the length by the width.

Geometry in the World

Geometry is everywhere! Architects use it to design buildings, artists use it to create beautiful pictures, and even nature uses it to form honeycombs and spider webs.

Geometry helps us see the world in a new way and understand how everything fits together.

Fractals

What Are Fractals?

Fractals are special patterns that look the same no matter how close you zoom in.

Imagine you have a picture of a tree. If you zoom in on a branch, it looks a bit like the whole tree.

If you zoom in even more on a smaller branch, it still looks like the whole tree. This repeating pattern is what makes something a fractal.

Let's start with a simple example called the Sierpinski Triangle.

1. Big Triangle: Start with a big triangle.

2. Smaller Triangles: Draw a dot in the middle of each side and connect these dots to make four smaller triangles.

3. Remove the Middle Triangle: Take out the middle triangle.

4. Repeat: Now, do the same thing to the three remaining triangles. Draw dots in the middle of each side, connect them, and remove the middle triangles

You keep repeating this process, and each time you get a pattern that looks like lots of little triangles making up the big triangle. No matter how much you zoom in, you see the same pattern.

Fractals in Nature

Fractals aren't just in math; they're everywhere in nature! Here are a few examples:

- Broccoli: Look at a piece of broccoli. Each small piece looks like a tiny version of the whole broccoli. Just because they are yucky doesn't mean they can't be mathematically interesting!

- Snowflakes: Snowflakes have intricated, repeating patterns that look similar at different scales.

- Coastlines: If you look at a map of a coastline, it looks jagged and irregular. Zooming in on a small part of the coastline still shows a similar jagged pattern.

Why Fractals Are Cool in Math

Fractals are fascinating in math because they help us understand complex shapes and patterns. They show us that simple rules can create incredibly detailed and beautiful designs. Here's why they're important:

Infinite Detail: Fractals can have an infinite amount of detail. No matter how much you zoom in, there's always more to see.

Self-Similarity: Fractals look the same at different scales. This property is called self-similarity.

Simple Rules, Complex Results: Fractals show how simple mathematical rules can create complex and beautiful patterns.

Fun with Fractals

You can even create your own fractals! Try drawing a simple shape and then repeat a pattern inside it, just like with the Sierpinski Triangle. Keep going as long as you can, and you'll see how a simple rule can make a complex and interesting design.

Fractals are a wonderful way to see how math creates patterns and structures all around us. They help us understand nature, art, and many other things in the world. Plus, they're just plain fun to look at and explore!

Benoit B Mandelbrot is the person who gave fractals their name

Joke:

What does the B in Benoit B Mandelbrot stand for?

Benoit B Mandelbrot! It's a fractal!

#10

#11
Pi (π) is Infinite

Pi (π) is a very special number that represents the ratio of a circle's circumference to its diameter.

What's amazing about π is that it never ends and never repeats. The first few digits are 3.14159, but it goes on forever!

3.14159265358979323846
02884197169399375106582
097816640628620899862803

π

What is Pi?

Pi (π) is a special number used in math to help us understand circles. It is the number you get when you divide the distance around a circle (the circumference) by the distance across the circle (the diameter). No matter how big or small the circle is, this number is always the same.

The Number Pi

When we write down Pi, it starts like this: 3.14159... and goes on and on. But here's the cool part: it never stops, and it never repeats the same pattern. It's like a story that goes on forever without ever repeating any part of it exactly the same way.

Why is Pi Infinite?

1. Endless Counting: Think about counting numbers. You can count forever: 1, 2, 3, 4, and so on. There's no end. Pi is a bit like that, but with digits after the decimal point.

2. No Repeating Pattern: Some numbers, like 1/3, have repeating patterns (0.333...). But Pi isn't like that. It doesn't have any repeating pattern no matter how far you go. It's like writing a story with no repeated sentences.

3. Finding Pi: To find the digits of Pi, mathematicians use special formulas and computers. They have found millions of digits of Pi, and it still keeps going without repeating!

A Fun Way to Think About Pi

Imagine you have a really long piece of string, and you start wrapping it around a circle. No matter how long you keep wrapping, you'll always be able to keep measuring more and more precisely how many times that string goes around the circle. The number you get, Pi, will keep going on and on.

So, Pi is an endless number that helps us understand circles, and its never-ending digits make it one of the coolest numbers in math!

Zero is an Even Number

What is an Even Number?

An even number is any number that can be divided by 2 without leaving any leftovers. For example, if you have 4 cookies and you want to share them with a friend, you can give each of you 2 cookies, and there are no cookies left over. So, 4 is an even number.

What is Zero?

Zero means you have nothing at all. If you have zero cookies, it means you don't have any cookies to share.

How Do We Know Zero is Even?

Let's see if zero can be divided by 2 without any leftovers.: If you have zero cookies and you want to share them with your friend, you would each get zero cookies. There are no cookies left over, right? So, zero can be divided by 2.

Think of a number line with both positive and negative numbers. Even numbers are usually marked in a different colour. If you look closely, you'll see that zero is right in between the positive and negative even numbers, like -2, -4, 2, 4, and so on.

Since even numbers follow a simple rule (can be divided by 2 without leftovers), zero fits this rule perfectly. Zero divided by 2 is zero, and there are no leftovers.

Cool Fact!

Every even number has a twin:

2 has -2
4 has -4

Zero has itself because zero is in the middle of all even numbers. It makes zero extra special!

The same is true for odd numbers

#12

The Number 0.999...

Let's explore how the number 0.999... (with the 9s going on forever) is actually the same as 1 using a fun trick with algebra.

Conclusion

We started by saying

x=0.999... and ended up finding that x=1.

This means that 0.999... (with the 9s going on forever) is actually the same as 1!

It's a neat trick that shows how sometimes numbers can be a little surprising.

Let's say

x is the number 0.999... (where the 9s go on forever).

So, we can write:

x = 0.999...

Multiply by 10:

If we multiply both sides of the equation by 10, we get:

10x=9.999....

Now we have two equations:

x=0.999... and 10x=9.999...

Subtract the first equation from the second:

Let's subtract x=0.999... from 10x=9.999...:

10x−x=9.999...−0.999....

Simplify the subtraction:

On the left side,

10x−x is 9x

On the right side,

9.999...−0.999... is exactly 9 (since the repeating parts cancel each other out).

So, we get: 9x=9. Solve for x

To find x, we divide both sides of the equation by 9: x =1

#14

Fibonacci Sequence in Nature

What is the Fibonacci Sequence?

The Fibonacci Sequence is a special list of numbers that starts like this:

1, 1, 2, 3, 5, 8, 13, 21, 34, ...

To get the next number in the sequence, you add the two numbers before it:

- 1 + 1 = 2

- 1 + 2 = 3

- 2 + 3 = 5

- 3 + 5 = 8

- And so on...

How Does the Fibonacci Sequence Appear in Nature?

Nature loves the Fibonacci Sequence! Here are some cool examples:

Flower Petals

Many flowers have a number of petals that is a Fibonacci number. For example, lilies have 3 petals, buttercups have 5 petals, and daisies often have 34 or 55 petals.

Pinecones:

If you look at a pinecone, you'll see that the scales are arranged in spirals. Count the spirals in one direction, and you'll find a Fibonacci number. Count in the opposite direction, and you'll find the next Fibonacci number!

Sunflowers

Sunflower seeds are arranged in spirals too. If you count the spirals, you'll often find Fibonacci numbers. This pattern helps the seeds pack tightly and efficiently.

Leaf Arrangements

Some plants grow their leaves in a spiral pattern around the stem. If you count the number of leaves in one full turn around the stem, you'll often find a Fibonacci number. This arrangement helps the leaves get the most sunlight.

Shells

The shells of some snails and sea creatures follow a spiral pattern that grows wider in a way described by the Fibonacci Sequence. This helps the animal grow evenly and efficiently.

Why Does Nature Use the Fibonacci Sequence?

Nature uses the Fibonacci Sequence because it helps plants and animals grow in the most efficient way possible. For example:

- The arrangement of leaves helps plants get the most sunlight.

- The pattern of seeds in a sunflower helps them pack tightly without wasting space

Fun Activity

You can find Fibonacci numbers in nature yourself!

Next time you're outside, look at flowers, pinecones, or even a snail shell. Count the petals, spirals, or sections, and see if you find a Fibonacci number.

Nature uses these patterns because they help plants and animals grow efficiently and beautifully. It's like nature's secret code for making things work perfectly!

ISN'T IT AMAZING HOW MATH IS HIDDEN ALL AROUND US IN NATURE?

The Golden Ratio

Where Does the Golden Ratio Show Up?

In Shapes and Art

Imagine a rectangle that is longer and thinner. If you cut off a square from one end, the remaining rectangle will have the same proportions as the original one. That rectangle's length to its width is the Golden Ratio.

In Nature

 - The Golden Ratio shows up in many living things. For example, it can be seen in the spiral pattern of a seashell or the way leaves are arranged on a stem. Even the proportions of your own body, like the length of your arm bones compared to your hand, can follow the Golden Ratio!

In Architecture

Architects sometimes use the Golden Ratio when designing buildings because it's pleasing to the eye. Ancient Greek temples, like the Parthenon, were built using these proportions.

People like the Golden Ratio because it looks balanced and beautiful. When things are built or designed using these proportions, they often seem just right to us.

Understanding the Golden Ratio helps us see how math and beauty can go hand in hand. You might be surprised where you find it next!

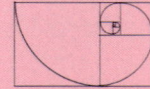

The Golden Ratio is a special number that people have been fascinated with for a long time.

It's about 1.618, and it's often represented by the Greek letter φ (phi).

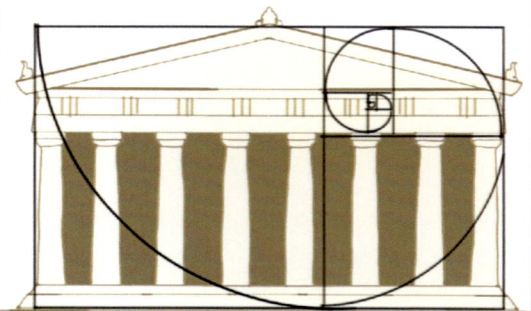

#15

Hexagons are Efficient

Let's talk about why hexagons are so cool and why bees use them to build their honeycombs.

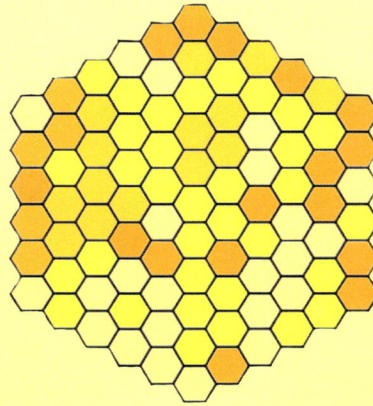

16

Imagine you have a bunch of shapes, like squares, triangles, and hexagons.

If you want to cover a flat surface with these shapes without leaving any gaps, some shapes do a better job than others.

Squares and triangles fit together without gaps, but hexagons are even better because they cover the most area with the least amount of edges.

Efficiency:

Bees are super smart when it comes to building their homes, called honeycombs.

They use hexagons because this shape is the most efficient for a few reasons:

Uses the Least Material: Hexagons use the least amount of wax to create their honeycomb cells. This means bees can save their energy and resources.

Strong and Sturdy: The hexagon shape makes the honeycomb strong, so it can hold lots of honey without breaking.

When hexagons are placed next to each other, there are no gaps. This makes the honeycomb very efficient in using space.

Imagine you're drawing a bunch of circles that all touch each other. The spaces in between these circles form a shape, and that shape is a hexagon!

Think of a soccer ball pattern. The patches on a soccer ball are made up of hexagons (and a few pentagons). They fit together nicely without any spaces.

Bees need to store their honey and raise their young in a space that's strong, uses the least amount of resources, and fits together perfectly.

By using hexagons, bees can build a large, strong honeycomb using less wax, leaving more energy for making honey.

So, next time you see a bee or a honeycomb, you'll know that those hexagons are a super smart choice for building a strong and efficient home!

Logic Gates and Dominoes

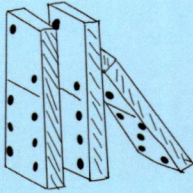

#17

Logic gates are like little machines that help computers make decisions. They take in signals (which can be thought of as yes or no, or on or off) and give out a new signal based on some rules.

Imagine you have a bunch of dominoes. If you set them up in a line and push the first one, they'll all fall down, right? We can use this idea to make logic gates!

AND Gate

An AND gate works like this: it only gives an "on" signal (or lets the dominoes fall) if all the inputs are "on". Imagine two lines of dominoes that meet at a single domino. Both lines need to be pushed at the same time for that meeting domino to fall and continue the chain.

OR Gate

An OR gate gives an "on" signal if at least one of the inputs is "on". Think of it as having two lines of dominoes leading to a single domino. If you push either line, the single domino will fall.

NOT Gate

A NOT gate is a bit different. It changes the signal from "on" to "off" or from "off" to "on". Imagine a domino setup where if you push one line of dominoes, it knocks over another line that prevents the final domino from falling. So, if the first line falls, the final domino doesn't; if the first line doesn't fall, the final domino will fall.

By combining these simple setups with dominoes, you can create more complex machines that can solve all sorts of problems, just like how computers work!

Logic gates are closely related to math because they follow specific rules that are part of a branch of math called "Boolean algebra." Boolean algebra is all about working with true and false values, which we can think of as yes and no, or 1 and 0.

AND Gate and Math

In math terms, an AND gate works like multiplication. If we think of "on" as 1 and "off" as 0:

- 1 AND 1 = 1 (both inputs are "on," so the output is "on")

- 1 AND 0 = 0 (one input is "off," so the output is "off")

- 0 AND 1 = 0 (one input is "off," so the output is "off")

- 0 AND 0 = 0 (both inputs are "off," so the output is "off")

OR Gate and Math

An OR gate works like addition, but with a twist. In Boolean algebra, 1 + 1 is still 1 because it's like saying "either one or the other or both are true":

- 1 OR 1 = 1 (at least one input is "on," so the output is "on")

- 1 OR 0 = 1 (at least one input is "on," so the output is "on")

- 0 OR 1 = 1 (at least one input is "on," so the output is "on")

- 0 OR 0 = 0 (both inputs are "off," so the output is "off")

NOT Gate and Math

A NOT gate just flips the value. If it's 1 (on), it turns into 0 (off), and if it's 0 (off), it turns into 1 (on):

- NOT 1 = 0

- NOT 0 = 1

When you set up dominoes to act like these gates, you're creating physical representations of these math rules. By combining these rules, you can make really complex calculations and decisions, just like how a computer does math to solve problems.

SO, BUILDING LOGIC GATES WITH DOMINOES IS LIKE PLAYING WITH MATH IN A FUN AND PHYSICAL WAY!

#18
What is e?

The number e is a special number in math, just like π (pi). It's about 2.718, but it goes on forever without repeating.

e is an important number in math, especially in areas like calculus and exponential growth.

Cool Facts About e

1. Natural Exponential Growth:

Think about a tree growing or money in a savings account earning interest. These kinds of things grow in a special way that uses the number □

2. Euler's Discovery:

A Swiss mathematician named Leonhard Euler discovered □ in the 1700s. He found it when he was studying how things grow continuously, like how bacteria multiply or how interest on money adds up.

3. The Magic of Compounding:

If you put money in a bank, the interest can add up in a magical way. The more often the interest is added (compounded), the closer it gets to growing by the number e

Euler's Formula:

There's a super cool equation called Euler's formula that connects □, π, and imaginary numbers. It looks like this:

$$e^{i\pi}+1=0$$

This equation is amazing because it connects some of the most important numbers in math!

Never-Ending Number:Just like π, e never ends and never repeats. The first few digits are 2.71828, but it keeps going forever.

Fun Example

Imagine you have $1 and you put it in a bank that gives you 100% interest, but they add the interest continuously. After one year, you wouldn't just have $2, you'd have about $2.718 because of the special way □ works.

Why e is Special

The number e helps us understand and calculate things that grow or change continuously. Whether it's the way populations grow, how heat spreads, or even how we calculate probabilities in games, □ is there making things work smoothly.

So next time you hear about exponential growth or see a cool math trick, remember that the number e is often behind the scenes making it all happen!

#19

Let's play a fun game with numbers and learn something cool about the number e!

LET'S PLAY!

The Game

Get a Random Number Generator:

You can use an online random number generator or write numbers 1 to 100 on slips of paper and draw them from a hat.

Start Generating Numbers:

Start generating random numbers between 1 and 100. Each time you generate a number, add it to your total.

Keep Going Until You Reach 100 or More:

Keep generating and adding numbers until your total is 100 or more.

Count Your Tries:

Count how many numbers it took to reach 100 or more.

Playing the Game

Let's say you play the game a few times. Here's what it might look like:

First try: You generate numbers 10, 20, 30, 40 (total = 100). It took 4 tries.

Second try: You generate numbers 50, 20, 20, 15 (total = 105). It took 4 tries.

Third try: You generate numbers 5, 10, 15, 30, 40 (total = 100). It took 5 tries.

How It Works

Randomness and Averages:

When you generate random numbers, each number can be anything from 1 to 100. The average number you generate will be around 50, but because you stop as soon as the total reaches or exceeds 100, the actual count of tries tends to follow a pattern that relates to e

More Tries, More Accuracy:

The more times you play the game and average the results, the closer you get to seeing this pattern. It's like flipping a coin many times; the more you do it, the closer you get to an even split of heads and tails.

Why It's Fun

This game is fun because it combines randomness and a bit of math magic. You get to see a special number, □ in action just by playing and counting. Plus, it's a great way to understand how certain patterns and averages appear naturally in numbers.

So, gather your random number generator and start playing!

See how close you can get to □ by averaging the number of tries it takes to reach 100 or more. Enjoy discovering the magic of math in a fun and interactive way!

Number Bases

20

What Are Number Bases?

Number bases are like different ways of counting. The most common way we count is called "base 10" (also known as the decimal system), which uses ten digits: 0, 1, 2, 3, 4, 5, 6, 7, 8, and 9. But there are other ways to count, too, using different bases.

Base 10 (Decimal)

Let's start with base 10 since it's the one we use every day. Here's how it works:

- When you count, you start at 0 and go up to 9.

- After 9, you go back to 0 but add a 1 in front, making 10.

- This pattern continues: 11, 12, 13, and so on.

The place value of each digit in a number tells you how much it's worth. In the number 345:

- The 5 is in the "ones" place (5 ones).

- The 4 is in the "tens" place (4 tens, or 40).

- The 3 is in the "hundreds" place (3 hundreds, or 300).

Base 16 (Hexadecimal)

Another interesting base is base 16, called hexadecimal. It uses sixteen digits: 0, 1, 2, 3, 4, 5, 6, 7, 8, 9, and then A, B, C, D, E, and F (where A is 10, B is 11, and so on).

- When you count, you start at 0 and go up to F.

- After F, you go back to 0 but add a 1 in front, making 10 (which is 16 in decimal).

- This pattern continues: 11 (which is 17 in decimal), 12, 13, ..., 1F, 20 (which is 32 in decimal), and so on.

Base 2 (Binary)

Now let's look at base 2, which is called binary. Computers use this system. It only has two digits: 0 and 1.

- When you count, you start at 0 and go up to 1.

- After 1, you go back to 0 but add a 1 in front, making 10 (which is 2 in decimal).

- This pattern continues: 11 (which is 3 in decimal), 100 (which is 4 in decimal), and so on.

The place value works differently in binary. In the number 101:

- The 1 on the right is in the "ones" place (1 one).

- The 0 is in the "twos" place (0 twos, or 0).

- The 1 on the left is in the "fours" place (1 four).

So, 101 in binary is 1 four + 0 twos + 1 one, which equals 5 in decimal.

How Different Bases Are Used

- Base 10: Used in everyday life for counting and calculations.

- Base 2: Used by computers and digital systems because they operate with two states: on and off.

- Base 16: Used in computing to represent binary numbers more compactly.

Fun with Bases

Here's a fun way to think about it: Imagine you're playing a game and you can only use a certain number of fingers to count. In base 10, you use all ten fingers. In base 2, you can only use two fingers (0 and 1). In base 16, you get to use your fingers and toes plus some extra digits!

By exploring different bases, you can see how numbers work in various systems, which helps us understand and create amazing things like computers and digital gadgets. It's like having a secret code for counting!

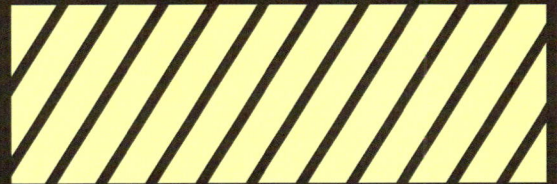

21

The Riemann Hypothesis is another fascinating puzzle in the world of math. Imagine it like this:

You know about numbers, right? Numbers like 1, 2, 3, 4, and so on. There's a special kind of number called a prime number. A prime number is a number that can only be divided by 1 and itself without any leftovers. For example, 2, 3, 5, 7, and 11 are all prime numbers.

Now, imagine you have a magical number line where all the numbers are lined up. There's a special function called the "Riemann Zeta Function" that helps mathematicians understand the prime numbers and how they are spread out along this number line.

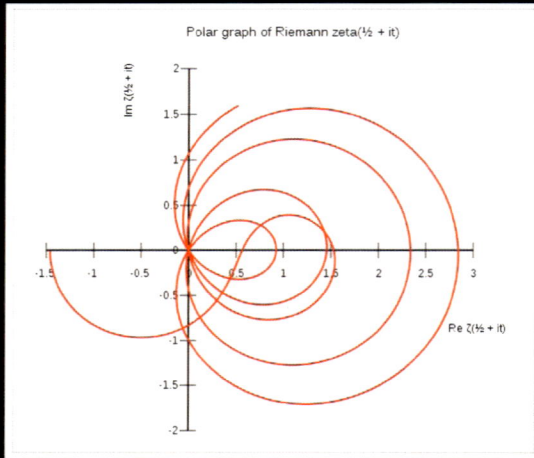
Polar graph of Riemann zeta(½ + it)

The Riemann Hypothesis

The Riemann Hypothesis is like a guess about this magical function. It says that there is a special pattern to the prime numbers when you use this function. Specifically, the Riemann Hypothesis suggests that all the interesting points (called "zeros") of this function, where the magic kind of happens, are lined up in a certain way on the number line.

Imagine drawing a straight line through the middle of a piece of paper, and all these special points are supposed to sit exactly on this line. If they do, it means we understand a lot about how prime numbers work and where they are.

The Riemann Hypothesis is still a mystery because even though many of these special points have been found on the line, no one has been able to prove that all of them are on the line.

SOLVING THIS WOULD BE A HUGE BREAKTHROUGH IN MATH!

Goldbach Conjecture

The Goldbach Conjecture is a very old and interesting math puzzle. It's named after a man named Christian Goldbach who thought of it a long time ago.

Here's the idea:

You know about even numbers, right? Even numbers are numbers like 2, 4, 6, 8, 10, and so on. They're all numbers that you can split into two equal parts without any leftovers.

The Goldbach Conjecture says that every even number that is bigger than 2 can be written as the sum of two prime numbers.

Now, prime numbers are special numbers that can only be divided by 1 and themselves without any leftovers. Some examples of prime numbers are 2, 3, 5, 7, and 11.

So, let's try this with an example:

Take the even number 8. According to the Goldbach Conjecture, we should be able to write 8 as the sum of two prime numbers. And we can! 8 = 3 + 5 (both 3 and 5 are prime numbers).

Another example: take the even number 10. We can write 10 as 5 + 5, and both 5s are prime numbers.

Goldbach's Conjecture says this should work for every even number bigger than 2, but no one has been able to prove this for all even numbers yet. It's like a big math mystery that mathematicians are still trying to solve!

#22

Twin prime conjecture

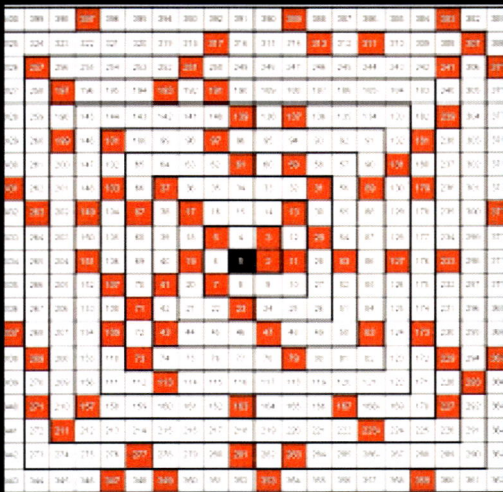

23

Let's talk about the Twin Prime Conjecture.

You know what prime numbers are, right? They are special numbers that can only be divided by 1 and themselves. Examples of prime numbers are 2, 3, 5, 7, 11, 13, and so on.

Now, let's talk about twin primes. Twin primes are pairs of prime numbers that are just 2 numbers apart.

For example:

3 and 5 are twin primes because they are both prime and the difference between them is 2.

11 and 13 are twin primes for the same reason.

17 and 19 are another pair of twin primes.

The Twin Prime Conjecture is a puzzle that mathematicians are trying to solve. It asks whether there are infinitely many pairs of twin primes. This means, as you count up higher and higher, will you keep finding pairs of prime numbers that are only 2 numbers apart, forever?

So far, mathematicians have found lots and lots of twin primes, but they haven't been able to prove that you can always find more twin primes no matter how high you go. It's like a mystery in math where we know some of the clues but haven't found the final answer yet.

Collatz Conjecture

Let's talk about the Collatz Conjecture, which is like a fun math game with numbers.

Here's how the game works:

1. Pick any positive number you like. Let's call this number your "starting number."

2. If your number is even (like 2, 4, 6), you divide it by 2.

3. If your number is odd (like 1, 3, 5), you multiply it by 3 and then add 1.

4. Take the new number you get and repeat the steps above.

The Collatz Conjecture says that no matter what number you start with, if you keep following these steps, you'll always eventually reach the number 1.

Let's try an example with the starting number 6:

6 is even, so we divide by 2 and get 3.

3 is odd, so we multiply by 3 and add 1, getting 10.

10 is even, so we divide by 2 and get 5.

5 is odd, so we multiply by 3 and add 1, getting 16.

16 is even, so we divide by 2 and get 8.

8 is even, so we divide by 2 and get 4.

4 is even, so we divide by 2 and get 2.

2 is even, so we divide by 2 and get 1.

And we reached 1!

The puzzle (Collatz Conjecture) is whether this game will always end at 1, no matter what number you start with. Mathematicians have tested lots of numbers and it always seems to work, but no one has been able to prove it for every possible number yet. So it's a big, interesting mystery in math!

Fun fact: 27 takes 111 steps to complete its Collatz sequence

#24

Let's learn a cool trick to multiply big numbers that are close to 100, like 98 and 97. This trick will make you feel like a math magician!

Imagine you want to multiply 98 and 97. Here's how you can do it quickly and easily:

Subtract each number from 100:

Take 98 and subtract it from 100:

100−98=2.

Take 97 and subtract it from 100:

100−97=3.

Multiply the two differences we found:

2×3=6.

Subtract the sum of the differences from 100:

Add the differences together:

2+3=5.

Subtract this sum from 100:

100−5=95.

Combine the results:

Put together the 95 and the 6 to give us 9506.

So,

98×97=9506!

Multiplying Large Numbers

X

Why This Works

This trick works because of some neat properties of numbers and how they interact. When you subtract the numbers from 100, you're essentially breaking down the multiplication into simpler steps.

This trick shows how fascinating and beautiful math can be! With just a few simple steps, you can multiply large numbers quickly and impress your friends and family with your math skills.

#25

#26

Magic Squares

What is a Magic Square?

A magic square is a special kind of puzzle that's like a magic trick with numbers. It's a grid (like a box) filled with numbers where each row, column, and diagonal adds up to the same number. That number is the magic number!

15	10	3	6
4	5	16	9
14	11	2	7
1	8	13	12

How Does It Work?

Grid with Numbers

Imagine a 3x3 grid (a square with 3 rows and 3 columns).

You fill this grid with numbers, like this:

```
4 9 2

3 5 7

8 1 6
```

Magic Sum

Now, add up the numbers in each row, column, and diagonal:

- Row 1: 4 + 9 + 2 = 15

- Row 2: 3 + 5 + 7 = 15

- Row 3: 8 + 1 + 6 = 15

Magic Number

In this example, the magic number is 15! That means every line you draw (across, up and down, and diagonally) will always add up to 15.

Why is it Magic?

Magic squares are like puzzles because you can make different squares with different numbers, but they all have the same magic number. It's like a cool trick with numbers that always works out the same way.

Fun Fact:

There are bigger magic squares, like 4x4 grids (4 rows and 4 columns) or even 5x5 grids! They work the same way—every row, column, and diagonal adds up to the same number.

TRY IT YOURSELF

You can create your own magic square! Just remember, all the numbers have to add up to the same magic number in every direction. It's a fun way to play with numbers and see how they fit together like a puzzle!

Magic squares are a neat way to see how numbers can make patterns that are surprising and fun!

#27

Math Tricks

HERE ARE A FEW FUN MATH TRICKS THAT YOU CAN EASILY LEARN AND IMPRESS YOUR FRIENDS WITH.

Trick 1: The 9 Times Table Trick

Have you ever noticed how the 9 times table has a cool pattern? Here's a simple way to remember it:

1. Write down the numbers 0 to 9 in order:

   - 0, 1, 2, 3, 4, 5, 6, 7, 8, 9

2. Next to them, write the numbers 9 to 0 in reverse order:

   - 9, 8, 7, 6, 5, 4, 3, 2, 1, 0

Now, read the pairs of numbers together, and you get:

- 09 (which is 9 x 1)

- 18 (which is 9 x 2)

- 27 (which is 9 x 3)

- 36 (which is 9 x 4)

- 45 (which is 9 x 5)

- 54 (which is 9 x 6)

- 63 (which is 9 x 7)

- 72 (which is 9 x 8)

- 81 (which is 9 x 9)

- 90 (which is 9 x 10)

Cool, right?

Trick 2: The Magic Number 1089

This is a fun trick that works every time!

1. Think of a three-digit number where the first and last digits are different (like 421).

2. Reverse the number (124).

3. Subtract the smaller number from the bigger number (421 - 124 = 297).

4. Now, reverse the result (792).

5. Add the result to the reversed number (297 + 792).

The answer will always be 1089!

Trick 3: Multiplying by 11

Here's an easy way to multiply any two-digit number by 11.

1. Take a two-digit number (let's use 34).

2. Separate the digits (3 and 4).

3. Add the two digits together (3 + 4 = 7).

4. Place the sum in between the two digits of the original number (3 _ 4 becomes 374).

So, 34 x 11 = 374.

Note: If the sum of the digits is more than 9, just carry over the extra. For example:

- 57 x 11: 5 + 7 = 12, so put 2 in the middle and add 1 to 5: 627.

Math Tricks continued

Trick 4: The Disappearing Dollar Trick

This is a fun puzzle rather than a trick, but it's great for thinking!

Three friends go to a restaurant and share a meal costing $30. Each pays $10. The waiter realizes there's a mistake and the meal should have cost $25, so he gives $5 back. The friends decide to take $1 each and give $2 as a tip. Now, each friend has paid $9 (because they got $1 back from the $10, they originally paid), so $9 x 3 = $27. Plus, the $2 tip makes $29. Where did the missing dollar go?

The trick here is in how the math is being added up. There is no missing dollar. They paid $27, which includes the $25 for the meal and the $2 tip.

Trick 5: Mind-Reading Number Trick

1. Think of a number (let's use 5).

2. Double it (5 x 2 = 10).

3. Add 8 (10 + 8 = 18).

4. Divide by 2 (18 / 2 = 9).

5. Subtract the original number (9 - 5 = 4).

No matter what number you start with, the answer will always be 4!

These tricks are a fun way to play with numbers and see some of the patterns and surprises in math!

MATH

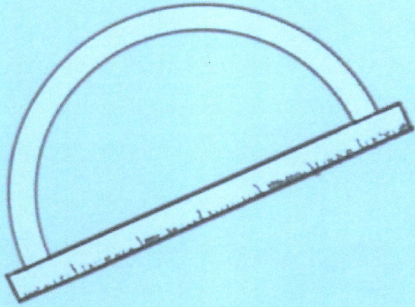

IS PRETTY AMAZING, DON'T YOU THINK?

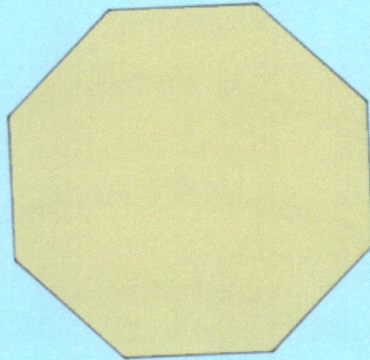

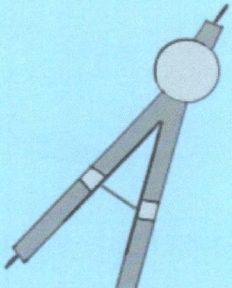

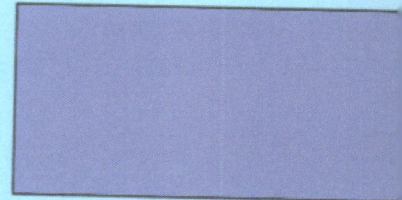

28

Perfect Numbers

A perfect number is a number that is equal to the sum of its proper divisors (excluding itself). For example, the number 6 is perfect because its divisors are 1, 2, and 3, and 1 + 2 + 3 = 6.

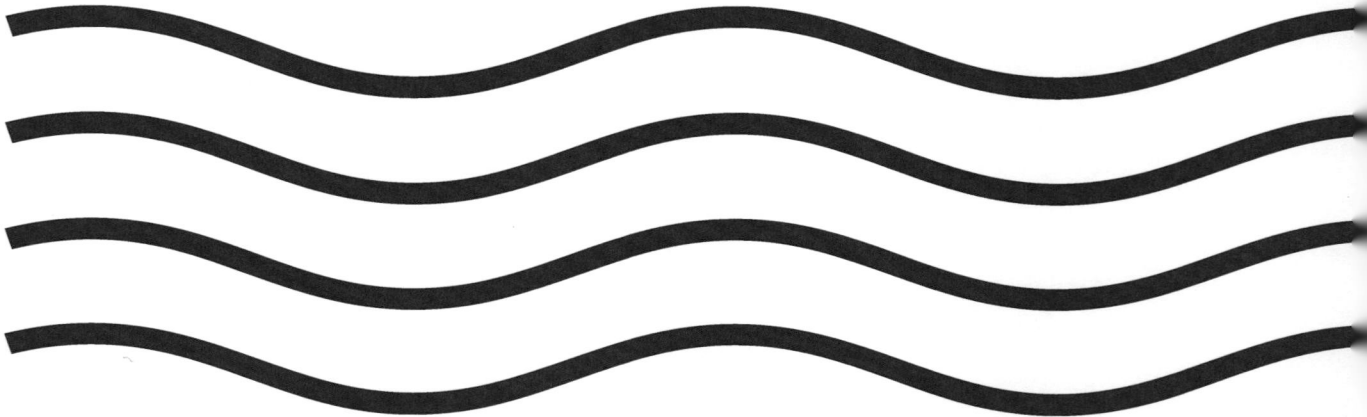

Imagine you have a bunch of friends, and you want to share something with them equally. Let's say you have 28 pieces of candy. You want to see if you can share these candies with your friends in such a way that everyone gets the same amount, and there's nothing left over.

A perfect number is a special kind of number that can be split up exactly like this, using its own pieces. Here's how it works:

First, find all the numbers that can divide the perfect number without leaving any pieces left over. These are called divisors.

Add up all these divisors (but don't include the number itself).

If the sum of these divisors equals the original number, then that number is perfect!

Let's see an example of this:

The number 28

Find the divisors of 28 (excluding 28 itself):

1 (because 28 divided by 1 is 28)

2 (because 28 divided by 2 is 14)

4 (because 28 divided by 4 is 7)

7 (because 28 divided by 7 is 4)

14 (because 28 divided by 14 is 2)

Add these divisors together: 1 + 2 + 4 + 7 + 14 = 28.

Since the sum is the same as the original number, 28 is a perfect number

Since the sum is the same as the original number, 28 is a perfect number!

So, perfect numbers are like magical numbers that can be split up perfectly into their own pieces!

Perfect!

#29

A fun math game.

Choose a number

Example: 12

Spell it out in English T-W-E-L-V-E

Count the letters – in this case it is 6

Spell it out in English S-I-X

Count out the letters

Keep going and see how long It takes you to get to 4 (it will always eventually get to 4)

Once you get to four it is impossible to get any other number except 4!

Do this with a friend and see who takes the longest to get to four.

#30 The final word count inside this book including this last fact is:

9668 words including numbers
1249 non-repeated words
51 089 characters with spaces
41 901 characters without spaces
624 paragraphs

This includes footnotes, textboxes and endnotes but not speech bubbles.

ISBN: 978-1-7637973-0-7

First Printed in 2024
©Copyright 1000 Tales.

Written by
Taarun Krushanth

Illustrated by
Ameera Karimshah and Atiya Karimshah

We would like to acknowledge the Traditional Custodians of the continent of Australia. Whose cultures are among the oldest living cultures in human history and whose languages and knowledge have infused and inhabited this land for millennia.

We recognise their continuing connection to the land, waters and culture and we pay our respects to their Elders past, present and emerging

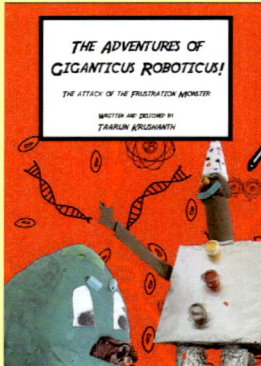

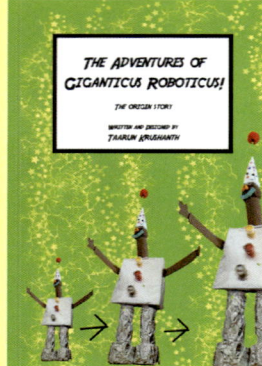

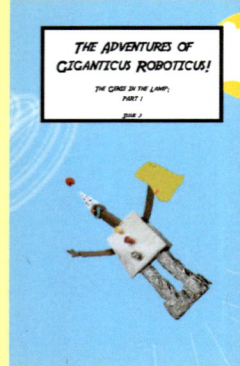

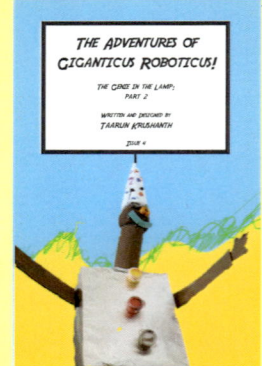